Women in rural development
The People's Republic of China

Women
in rural development

The People's Republic of China

International Labour Office   Geneva

ISBN 92-2-102054-1

First published 1979
Second impression 1980

Printed by the International Labour Office, Geneva, Switzerland

TABLE OF CONTENTS

PREFACE

This study forms part of the research work currently being undertaken by the Rural Employment Policies Branch on rural women in developing countries. The main objective of this programme is to increase our knowledge of the economic and social factors determining the conditions of life of rural women with emphasis on their participation in production and reproductive activities. Within this framework, the main areas of research interest are: (a) participation of women in the subsistence sector and family agricultural production, including sex roles and the actual division of labour in agricultural production, the extent of women's contribution to agriculture, and estimation of women's participation in the agricultural labour force; (b) women's participation in wage labour with a distinction between agricultural and non-agricultural wage labour; (c) the impact on rural women of agricultural organisation, including the ownership structure and output distribution; and (d) women's reproductive activities (bearing and caring of children and family maintenance) and its bearing on women's participation in productive activities.

It is hoped that results of this research will assist in the provision of guidelines for policy makers and planners concerned with the amelioration of working conditions and employment and income earning opportunities for women in rural areas. They should also influence the orientation of ILO's field and technical co-operation projects in the field of rural development.

The Chinese experience with its attempt to transform the social and economic conditions of women within a relatively short period of time should be of interest to all students of this subject. In this study, the author analyses the impact of various influences and policy measures on the situation of rural women in China. There is discussion of the efficacy of legislative measures to bring about equality for women. This is followed in turn by an analysis of the role of the productive system, ideology and women's movements in increasing the power, rights and independence of the rural women in China. Each of these factors has made a contribution in this regard but the author also brings out the constraints imposed by cultural influences and material conditions. The study concludes with a succinct summary of the main policy areas requiring attention and the relevance of the Chinese experience for other countries. The study makes a valuable contribution to a deeper understanding of the various mechanisms which sustain women's subordination. At the same time it highlights the point that even a revolutionary transformation of socio-economic structures may not suffice to bring about a state of equality for women.

Dharam Ghai
Chief
Rural Employment Policies Branch
Employment and Development Department

Author's note

I would like to take this opportunity to thank the International Labour Office for sponsoring this project and financing the research for this report. In particular, I am grateful to Ingrid Palmer, Lourdes Benería and Boo Ng for their interest and comments on both the initial proposals and drafts of this report. It is primarily based on documentary research undertaken in the British Library and the library of the School of Oriental and African Studies of the University of London and short periods of interviewing in the People's Republic itself. I would like to thank the Embassy of the People's Republic of China in London and the Travel Service in China for making these trips possible.

In this study I have mainly used the Hanyu Pinyin system of romanisation. The exceptions are composed of well-known place names, and where Chinese authors and titles have been written in or translated into English, then they remain as they were presented in the original texts.

There are two particular problems associated with the writing of this report to which I should like to draw attention. The first is that it is always difficult to present a short comprehensive study of women in a particular society while at the same time presenting adequate background material on the society itself. The first chapter attempts a brief survey of rural development in China, but for further information on the development process in China one issue of World Development (Vol. 3, Nos. 7 and 8, July-August 1975) is recommended. The second problem is to do with evaluating the development policies of China which are designed to end the subordination of women. This report both recognises and appreciates the tremendous changes in the conditions in which rural women live their lives, but at the same time it also discusses at length the problems entailed in such a process on the grounds that it is these which are particularly instructive to those involved in similar processes in other societies. The twists and turns in the experience of a society which is almost unique in the degree of conscious attention it has given to redefining the role of women cannot but be of interest and relevance to those involved in effecting similar changes elsewhere.

Elisabeth Croll,
London, March 1978.

List of abbreviations

ACDWF	All-China Democratic Women's Federation
CNA	China News Analysis, Hong Kong
CQ	China Quarterly, London
CR	China Reconstructs, Peking
FLP	Foreign Languages Press, Peking
GRB	Congren Ribao (Workers' Daily), Peking
KMRB	Guangming Ribao (Guangming Daily), Peking
NFRB	Nanfang Ribao (Nanfang Daily), Canton
NCNA	New China News Agency, London
PR	Peking Review, Peking
P's C	People's China, Peking
RMRB	Renmin Ribao (People's Daily), Peking
SWB	Survey of World Broadcasts, Far Eastern Section
ZF	Zhongguo Funu (Chinese Women), Peking
ZQ	Zhongguo Qingnian (China Youth), Peking

CHAPTER 1

Women and rural development in China

In examining the role and status of women within strategies of rural development, either in terms of their contribution to development or development's contribution to the total welfare of women, the People's Republic of China forms perhaps a unique and certainly a significant case study. It is a significant study because of the particular form which economic development or "modernisation" has taken, the scale on which the redefinition of the role and status of women has been attempted and because this process of social change has been the subject of conscious analysis within China for the past 25 years. As the Chinese themselves have said there is no blueprint for the emancipation or liberation of women[1] and they have found that as some old problems remain and other old problems are solved, new problems and new conditions for further development arise.[2] An examination of the strategies which have been adopted by China provides an opportunity to study a sequence of policies or the social processes by which one country has, over a period of time, consciously attempted to relate and integrate policies of rural development and policies to redefine the role and status of women.

This report briefly outlines the main characteristics of the development policies and the reorganisation of the rural sector since 1949, and analyses its effects on women's productive and reproductive activities.[3] It considers the strategies by which a

---

[1] RMRB (People's Daily), 8 Mar. 1973.

[2] Hongqi (Red Flag), 16 Apr. 1962.

[3] This report is based on a wide variety of sources. The materials generally fall into two categories: those to do with the policies as they have been introduced in China since 1949 and the assumptions on which they are based; and those to do with the implementation and practice of the policies. The former category includes both policy statements related to various stages in economic development and those specifically devoted to the role of women. Many of these are to be found in government source materials, authoritative articles and editorials in the press, educational materials in all their various forms and a study of the numbers of role models or public reference groups. To trace the development of these policies in practice and their implications for women the second category of source materials includes those case studies to be found in magazines, radio, newspapers and booklets, surveys and village and commune studies undertaken by Chinese and Western investigators. I myself was able to visit China in 1973 and in 1977 I was able to return and undertake a small field study in Guangdong Province. Because of the nature of the second category of materials it has not always been easy to provide quantifiable data of any substance or to make nation-wide generalisations, but it has been possible to suggest certain general patterns and trends of development, some regional variations and to delineate the problem areas.

traditionally oppressed group of low socio-economic status has been
assimilated into the economic and political activities of the public
domain and the effectiveness of the policies in attaining their
goals. The latter part of the report assesses the extent to which
both traditional and new ideological, economic and organisational
constraints presently inhibit the further redefinition of the
position of women in the rural sector. Although these concluding
sections are more concerned with understanding the operation of
certain mechanisms to do with the continuing subordination of women
in rural China, this report takes as axiomatic a recognition of the
benefits which the Chinese Government has brought to the rural
sector of the population. Over the last 20 years and for the first
time in their lives, almost all rural inhabitants have acquired a
new standard of living in the basic necessities - food, clothing,
housing, health care, education, culture and recreation. As many
observers have noted, collective enterprises, water control projects,
small industries, communication and distribution networks
characterise much of rural China. There can have been few parallel
rural transformations in such a short time span. The over-all
question to be examined in this report is to what extent women have
contributed to this development process and to what extent have
they shared in the benefits resulting from the rural transformation?

Policies of rural development

Rural development in China since 1949 has been based on
policies aimed at increasing and expanding agricultural production
and integrating agricultural policies within a broader socio-
economic development programme. China's development strategies
have been characterised by a heavy emphasis on the reorganisation[1]
of the relations of production, a number of pro-agrarian measures[1]
and an integrated approach centred primarily on the communes which
closely link agricultural production to distribution, rural capital
formation, rural industries and a wide range of social and welfare
activities. The transformation of rural life has been based on
socio-political as well as economic programmes and agricultural
policy itself has been based on a dual strategy of institutional
reforms and technological changes of the traditional rural economy.

Initially institutional changes were to take precedence over
any form of developmental changes including technological transformations on the grounds that in China it was the productive
relations which were impeding the development of the productive
forces. Throughout the 1950s the Chinese Government primarily
depended on institutional reorganisation to increase and expand
agricultural production. A number of policies were intended to
gradually collectivise the means of production and establish
collectives as units of production, distribution and consumption.
After land reform, or the redistribution of a certain amount of
land and tools of production, the Government encouraged individual
peasant households to pool labour and other means of production
much on the basis of traditional patterns of agricultural co-
operation. Many of these temporary or seasonal mutual aid teams

---

[1] Following an initial phase in the early 1950s which had
accorded agriculture a secondary position in relation to the
importance accorded to industrial growth, the Government in China
has consistently assigned a high priority to agricultural development.

became permanent institutions within the rural villages as they were incorporated into lower-stage co-operatives, consisting of 20 to 40 households and based on the principle of central management but private ownership. The income of the component households came from payment for labour services and payment for property contributed to the co-operative. Higher-stage co-operatives containing from 100 to 300 households were formed from the merger of a number of lower co-operatives and payments of dividends on land ceased. In 1958 these co-operatives were replaced by communes which became the basic economic unit of the countryside.

Rural people's communes developed out of the earlier experiments in agricultural reorganisation, but they differed from their fore-runners, the co-operatives, in that they were larger and they were not simply units of production. Instead they combined the responsi-bilities of government administration and the tasks of organising all production and services including health, education and defence. Initially each commune enjoyed a considerable measure of autonomy and the commune authority was the main unit of ownership and distri-bution with controls over the labour and material resources of the commune. But by the end of the first decade a three-tiered organisational form had been stabilised which comprised the commune and its constituent production brigades and production teams with the balance of authority in favour of the latter forms. The production brigade and production team, based on the whole of or part of the rural village depending on its size, became the basic unit of accounting, planning and distribution while the communes retained ownership of industrial plants and control over relations with state organs.

This reorganisation of the relations of production had certain implications for rural development programmes. First and foremost it enabled the collectives to mobilise and distribute the labour resources of the countryside. In China as in many Third World countries, underutilised resources of land and a ready supply of capital were not available on a wide scale, but the rural areas of China had traditionally been characterised by underemployed labour. As several agricultural economists have pointed out, the rural development strategy employed by China has above all demanded the utilisation of underemployed rural labour on a scale not attempted before in China or indeed elsewhere.[1] One economist has estimated that the creation of communes has made it possible to increase the labour inputs in agriculture at three to four times the prewar level.[2] The institutional transformation has not only allowed for a more intensive field cultivation, but also a degree of diversifi-cation of activities which have fully utilised the labour and material resources of the collectives. The Government anticipated that the collective possibilities for productive investment were greater than those for individual households and could potentially benefit all collective members. The collective was also more likely to effect a more rational management of agriculture by the pooling of small fragmented plots into larger units, and encouraged a certain expansion in subsidiary activities such as local industries,

---

[1] Chao Kuo-chun: Agrarian policy of the Communist Party, 1921-1959, London, 1960; U.D. Lippit: Land reform and economic development in China, New York, 1974; P. Schran: The development of Chinese agriculture, 1950-59, Chicago, 1969.

[2] J. Wong: Land reform in the People's Republic of China, New York, 1973.

handicrafts, livestock, fruit and vegetable growing, raising silk cocoons and fishing and the development of capital projects such as irrigation or water conservancy works, rural reconstruction projects, reclamation of wasteland and afforestation. Finally, it was likely that a number of collective services could be instituted such as grain processing, nurseries, sewing centres, medical services and a social security system which would provide for the welfare of its members.

Following the gradual reorganisation of the relations of production the priorities in rural development have shifted to technological reforms and the alteration of terms of trade between agriculture and industry in favour of agriculture and the peasants. Emphasis has been given to developing and introducing new agricultural techniques, the mechanisation of farm tools, irrigation, electrification, fertilization and seed breeding. The increase in capital goods and other inputs has been designed to expand the area of land given over to agricultural production through reclamation, conservation, multiple cropping and increasing the productivity of land by utilising better seeds, applying fertilizers, improving farm implements and reducing crop loss by controlling plant and animal pests. Finally, throughout most of the period the terms of trade have been steadily turning in favour of the peasants by the raising of prices paid by the State for agricultural products and the lowering of prices of many goods purchased by them.

This expansion in agricultural production and the diversification of rural activities has been planned on the assumption that China is uniquely rich in labour power and that women form one of the most underdeveloped of China's resources available for economic development. In the mid-1950s, Mao Tse-tung himself said of the role of China's women in the reorganisation and development of the countryside that they "form a vast reserve of labour power which should be tapped in the struggle to build a great socialist country".[1] Indeed, the planned expansion of agricultural production and the diversification of rural activities necessitated the inclusion of women in social production.

Women in rural development

Government policy, however, has not only assumed that the involvement of women in production was necessary for rural development, for it has also emphasised that involvement in production was of the utmost importance to the women themselves as a precondition for improvement in their own position in society. It predicted a direct correlation between participation in social production and their degree of control over economic resources and surplus. It assumed that entry into the wage labour force would enable women on the basis of their improved material conditions to acquire a new confidence, power and authority within the public and domestic spheres of society. Legislation designed to introduce equality and protect the rights of women might be a first step, but in 1949, participation in production was identified as the crucial breakthrough in winning these rights in practice.

---

[1] See The upsurge of socialism in the countryside, FLP, Peking, 1957, 286.

"... the mobilisation of women to participate in production is
the most important link in the chain that protects women's own
vital interests /... it is necessary to begin with production
for both economic prosperity and economic independence promote
the political status of women, their cultural level and improve
their livelihood, thereby leading the way to emancipation".[1]

On this basis successive government policies for the expansion and
reorganisation of production have both demanded the expansion of the
labour force to include women and provided new opportunities for
women to take a full and wide-ranging part in production. However
the total integration of women both as agents and as beneficiaries
into the rural development process demanded more than the encourage-
ment to enter into social production, important though that is.
For this reason it was part of a four-pronged strategy which aimed
to redefine both the legal and ideological definitions of women's
role and status and allowed for the development of a women's movement
to particularly forward their economic, social and political
interests.

/Soon after taking power in 1949 the national Government
promulgated the marriage and labour laws for the equality and
protection of women and children. In offering women institutionalised access to legal sanctions and an alternative power base
these laws allowed them the first opportunity to defy the authority
of the household head and directly contend his patriarchal
authority. / On the principle of the equality and protection of
women, the Marriage Law was designed to reduce the power of the men
of the family by altering patterns of inheritance and control over
children in favour of women and prohibiting the exchange of women
as a commodity. It increased the standing of the young bride
vis-à-vis her husband and her mother-in-law by introducing free
choice marriage thus strengthening the conjugal bond and protecting
the rights of women and children in the event of divorce. / The
Agrarian Reform Law gave women the right to own land and property
in their own name and the labour legislation allowed for the
equality of women with men in the labour force and provided for
maternity leave and benefits. The promulgation of these laws was
followed by extensive campaigns to make the new legal provisions
and facilities widely known and available throughout the country.
The limitations of law alone in affecting change had been all too
obvious in China following the promulgation of the 1930 Family Law
and it is an important point to note that such legislation did not
form the culmination of a campaign for women's rights, but was
indeed only the beginning of a much more intensive campaign to
redefine the position of women.

The Chinese Government has always emphasised that although it
was possible to alter the material basis of women's lives, it
should be realised quite clearly that customs and habits reflecting
the traditional subordination of women may remain, and it is the
struggle between new and old ideologies over the question of
marriage and family which is a matter of decisive importance.[2]

[1] Documents of the women's movement in China, ACDWF, 1949, 8.

[2] Yang Tawen and Liu Suping: "On the reform of our country's
system of marriage and the family", RMRB, 13 Dec. 1963.

To establish a new ideology incorporating new definitions of women to replace the traditional Confucian ideology advocating male supremacy and female subordination, secondariness and dependence, the Government encouraged a number of educational and consciousness-raising programmes to identify and criticise the remaining influence of the now outmoded code of ethics, proverbs and folk lore. Traditional ethical codes which taught that women should not concern themselves with public affairs and that disorder and disarray would follow if women were allowed to break this taboo were examined and criticised.   Women were encouraged to meet in small groups and break the tradition of silence or the "swallowing of their bitterness" and shed the mantle of dependence summed up in an old saying, "Marry a man, marry a man;   food to eat, clothes to wear".   In what became known as "speak bitterness meetings" they learned to articulate their own life histories and in an "exchange of experiences" they were urged to transform hidden individual fears and experiences into a shared awareness of the meaning of them as social problems.   Above all it was emphasised that the removal of norms of subordination required the conscious rejection of male supremacy and domination through language reform, the rewriting of educational texts and the nation-wide organisation of the subordinated to negotiate for themselves a new role and status in society.

Since its founding in 1921 the Communist Party of China had nurtured the separate organisation of women on the basis of their special experience of oppression and the necessity to form an independent power base from which women could conduct their struggle to protect and expand their new rights and opportunities in negotiating a new role and status.   In 1927 Mao Tse-tung first isolated the special oppression of women which identified them as a separate group in society.   In addition to the oppression shared by the men of their own social class, women also suffered a further oppression - that of male authority.[1]   The Chinese Communist Party also forecast that while a government could provide the legal and material conditions favourable to improvements in female status it was the women themselves who must be responsible for negotiating a new role in society, in converting new rights into new norms and practices and in setting new standards of social behaviour.   The new government might provide the necessary conditions, but in the last resort the struggle within individual families, villages and factories could only be carried out by the women themselves. Women then were to be encouraged to form their own solidarity groups to break down their traditional social isolation, and out of their shared concerns and common identity, the Government anticipated that women would acquire a power base which would enable them to actively negotiate a new role and status in the village.   On these two bases the Government sponsored the establishment of local groups of women as part of the nation-wide construction of the women's movement.

The Women's Federation was established in 1949 to strengthen the unity of women of all nationalities and classes, raise their levels of education and vocational skills, break down their traditional sense of isolation, support the newly won rights of women and give expression to their demands.[2]   Local groups centred

---

[1] See Selected works of Mao Tse-tung, Vol. I, pp. 44-46.

[2] Introducing the All-China Democratic Women's Federation, P's C, Mar. 1955.

on village neighbourhoods have taken a variety of forms such as
practical work teams, study groups and "exchange of experiences"
groups. Each plays a supporting role in meeting the practical and
emotional problems of its members and they elect representatives to
attend local women's conferences. The representative conference
is considered to be the local form of organisation most suited to
the conditions of rural and urban China, and throughout China
women's representative conferences have met periodically at the
various administrative levels from those of production brigade and
commune to province. The national congress of women is supposed
to meet every few years. The function of these conferences is to
discuss and summarise systematically the past policies of the
women's movement in the area represented and set forth new programmes of work. The national magazine has acted as a communica-
tions network between local groups and the women's movement is
encouraged to act as a pressure group watching over national and
local policies as they affect women.

Within the over-all strategy to effect rural development and
to redefine the position of women however the major government
policy has always been the entry of women into social production.
It was both necessary to the expansion and diversification of
production and for the redefinition of the position of women
themselves. Since this was the prior measure by which the
Government initially assessed its success in improving the position
of women, the next chapter examines in some detail the entry of
women into the agricultural labour force.

CHAPTER 2

Women in social production

In the 1940s and 1950s the Communist Party and Government introduced a number of policies and measures to encourage women to take part in agricultural production. Although peasant women had always laboured they had been mainly occupied by domestic production and reproduction, performed within the individual household. They primarily reared an animal or two and transformed raw materials for consumption and maintained the self-provisioning individual household and serviced its members. The most comprehensive data illustrating the percentage of farm work performed by peasant women before the 1940s and 1950s was that collated by the agricultural economist J.L. Buck in the early 1930s. In terms of work accomplished he estimated that men performed 80 per cent of all the farm labour in China, women 13 per cent and children seven per cent.[1] He also provided some impressions of the variations for different agricultural regions in China (see table 1).

Generally Buck's research indicates that the main contrast in the differential degree to which women perform field labour lies between the northern wheat-growing regions and the intensively cultivated southern rice regions. The largest proportion of labour contributed by women is in the double-cropping rice areas and the smallest is in the rice-tea and winter wheat-millet areas. However, throughout China with the exception of the southernmost rice-growing provinces, the proportion of field work undertaken by women is not great. It is likely that in all regions it is during the extremely busy seasons such as harvesting, when the labour supply became such a problem, that women were persuaded into the fields. J.L. Buck himself quotes a little ditty which supports this impression: "When it is busy on the farm, girls may leave their rooms to help".[2]

Individual village studies undertaken by social scientists before 1949 also substantiate this over-all impression. For instance, four of the studies in the southern rice region report that women took part in field work during the busy seasons of transplanting rice and the rice harvest.[3] Fei Hsiao-tung found in the villages of Yunnan Province (south-west rice area) that there was a clear division of labour. During the transplantation of rice, men pulled the shoots from the nursery beds and transported them and the women planted. Again at the rice harvest, women cut the grain, tied it and transported it to the threshing ground where

---

[1] J.L. Buck: Land utilisation in China, Nanking, 1937, pp. 291-2.

[2] J.L. Buck: op. cit., p. 307.

[3] D.M. Kulp: Country life in South China, Columbia, 1925, p. 96; C. Osgood: Village life in old China, New York, 1963, pp. 148-151; C.K. Yang: Communist society: The family and the village, MIT, 1959, p. 91.

Table 1:   The amount of farm labour and subsidiary work[1]
           performed by women (in percentages)

           (15,316 farms, 152 localities, 144 hsien, 22 provinces,
           China, 1929-31)

Regions and areas[2]	Proportion of farm work	Proportion of subsidiary work
CHINA (152)[3]	13	16
Wheat region (Nth China) (68)	9	15
Rice region (Sth China) (84)	16	17
WHEAT REGION AREAS:		
Spring wheat (13)	14	7
Winter wheat - millet (20)	5	25
Winter wheat - Kaoliang (35)	8	13
RICE REGION AREAS:		
Yangtze rice - wheat (31)	19	18
Rice - tea (22)	5	13
Szechwan rice (7)	11	21
Double-cropping rice (12)	29	14
South-western rice (12)	22	21

[1] The most common subsidary occupations are those of weaving, spinning, silk, livestock raising, merchant and professional occupations.

[2] See map on p. 10 for location of agricultural regions.

[3] Figures in brackets denote the number of localities researched in each region.

Source: J.L. Buck, Land utilisation in China, Nanking, 1937, pp. 293 and 297.

Agricultural regions of China as drawn by J.L. Buck

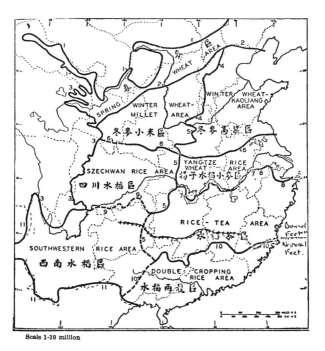

Scale 1-10 million

———————— Footbinding line

the men would thresh it.[1]   In the north of China the demands on
women's labour by the main crop, wheat, were much less.
A.H. Smith who made one of the very early studies of village life
in northern China reported that women rarely work in the cultivation of field crops, but at the time of the wheat harvest all
available women of the household helped to gather it in.[2] M. Yang,
who undertook a much later study in the winter wheat-millet region
also suggested that while women were not required to work in the
field in this region, they were frequently asked to thresh wheat
and millet and clean and cut sweet potatoes in the fields at
harvest time.[3]

The degree to which women contributed to agricultural production probably depended very much on the seasonal labour demands
made by the dominant and subsidiary crops and the timing or
coincidence of the peak labour demands of each.   It also depended
on the total human and animal resources of any given region.
For instance, there was more animal labour in the north of
China than in other regions where human labour was required
for pulling implements and carrying and transporting.
Where women were preoccupied by certain subsidiary and income-
earning occupations such as spinning and weaving and sericulture
they were less likely to work in the fields.   This was so in the
north of China, and in the Yangtze valley rice area, Fei Hsiao-tung
found there to be a clear division of labour between agriculture
and subsidiary occupations in this case silk cultivation which he
thought to be characteristic of such areas.   There, women were
entirely free from agriculture which was chiefly a man's occupation.[4]   The relatively low figures which Buck gives for women's
participation in subsidiary occupations may have been affected by
the degree to which they had suffered as a result of competition
from man-made fibres and machine goods.   For the Yangtze valley
area, Fei Hsiao-tung reported that due to the decline in the silk
industry women were now free to take part in agriculture.   But
their labour was only very occasionally required due to the fine
balance which had emerged between size of individual farms and
their male labour resources.[5]

Buck himself suggested that the amount of work performed by
women was partly associated with the extent to which feet were
bound, and therefore more women laboured in the southern rice
region than in the northern wheat region[6] (for line of footbinding

[1] Fei Hsiao-tung: Earthbound China, Chicago, 1945, p. 30.

[2] A.H. Smith: Village life in China, Edinburgh, 1900,
pp. 275-6.

3. M. Yang: A Chinese village: Tautou, Shantung Province,
Columbia, 1945, pp. 19 and 233.

[4] Fei Hsiao-tung: Peasant life in China, London, 1939, p. 170.

[5] ibid., p. 171.

[6] J.L. Buck: Land utilisation in China, Nanking, 1957, p. 292.
The physical mobility of most women in China in all but the most
southern of provinces was devastatingly affected by the practice of
footbinding whereby girls of seven and eight years of age had their
feet tightly wrapped and bent until the arch was broken and the toes
permanently bent under.   The degree to which feet were tightly
bound probably varied with each social class and peasant women
allowed a certain amount of agility in order to perform domestic chores.

see map on page 10).   However, bound feet seemed to have formed
less of a deterrent when women's labour was absolutely necessary.
In the spring wheat region where footbinding was very prevalent
and where it was so tight as to compel women to do their field
work on their knees, this did not prevent women undertaking
14 per cent of farm labour.[1]

Perhaps the most interesting factor in all these estimates is
that nowhere are the many household activities undertaken by women
quantified or even regarded as part of production.   For instance,
the transformation of raw material for consumption such as the
preparation of rice and cereals for cooking, the preserving and
drying of fruit, beans, seeds and vegetables took more time and
fell entirely within the women's sphere of labour and attention.
All the field studies completed in rural China in the early and
mid-twentieth century make reference to the time consumed in food
preparation, fuel gathering, the labour required for the making of
shoes, bedding and clothes and the depletion of women's physical
vitality due to the bearing and nursing of many infants.   The
larger proportion of women might seldom labour in the fields or in
what was defined as the productive sector, but they were far from
idle and serviced and maintained the household.

The mobilisation of women

The measures introduced by the new government in the 1950s
were designed to encourage women to take part in agricultural
production and overcome the prejudices which were likely to discourage them from taking up new occupations.   Women were generally
thought to be, and indeed often thought themselves to be, incapable
of acquiring the necessary skills and many were the superstitions
promising a certain evil or bad end to those who tried.   As one
women's leader in a co-operative said in 1953:

> You'd think it was easy, but it wasn't.   It was hard to
> enrol women in agricultural production.   The men declared:
> "Women are not farmers".   The older women said: "We can
> cook, make beds and hull grain.   We're no good in the
> fields".   Some of the younger women said they "also lacked
> the skill".[2]

In 1957, a nationwide document suggested that great efforts
were still needed to point out to both men and women why women's
labour was indispensable and a prerequisite to the expansion of
production.[3]   The men still had to be encouraged to get rid of
their usual contempt for women's working ability;   while the women
were to be urged yet further to give up their old ideas that production was men's work only.

Throughout the 1950s a combination of policies to specifically
encourage women to enter social production were introduced and
implemented:

---

[1] ibid.

[2] Shen Chilan: Women of New China, P's C, 16 Aug. 1953.

[3] See: Socialist upsurge in China, FLP, Peking, 1957, p. 287.

(a) In working out and establishing measures to encourage women to enter social production, steps were to be taken to consult and co-operate with the recently established local women's groups. They were to be assigned a major role in encouraging women to take part in social production. From the first women's groups were held responsible for the success or failure of village women to take up productive work.

> Women's groups should make their primary task the studying of how to organise village women to take part in individual and collective production work. They should help, aid and educate village women to solve their difficulties arising from their participation in production.[1]

They were exhorted to help women overcome their prejudices against working in the fields, acquire and master farming techniques and in turn act as a power base for rural women. Women's groups were to be responsible for reporting to the party committees and other relevant bodies, any recommendations and demands put forward by women. This was deemed to be one of their most important duties.[2]

(b) The separation of women into their own solidarity groups prior to entry into social production was carried through into the organisation of work groups within collective production units. Women were organised on a separate basis, not only in terms of separate work teams but in separate groups to whom experimental plots and new inputs might be given. It was conceived to be a matter of principle that the productive activities, quotas and achievements of women work teams be summed up separately in order to provide some incentive for the women and to overcome men's contempt for women's capabilities.[3] Steps were taken to encourage women, a disadvantaged group in the village, by giving them new inputs and encouraging them to set up rural experimental groups which were run and operated entirely by women. They might be encouraged by local research stations to try new seed strains, close planting, pest control, soil improvement, plant protection and fertilisation.[4] Very often the new methods might prove to be both feasible and successful and the results were to be summed up and popularised to provide a tangible measure of the independence and abilities of women to handle such tasks.[5]

---

[1] Documents of the women's movement, ACDWF, 1949, p. 3.

[2] Conference report of the ACDWF, RMRB, 20 Aug. 1959.

[3] See: Upsurge in socialist China, FLP, Peking, 1957, p. 276; Report of women's workteam, ZF, 1 Nov. 1961.

[4] NCNA, 7 Mar. 1959; PR, 10 Mar. 1961.

[5] Report from Yinxi Brigade, ZF, 1 Feb. 1966; NCNA, 4 Mar. 1976.

(c)   There was assumed to be a direct correlation between the quality of leadership of the women and the level of their activism and enthusiasm for social production.[1] Training courses were to be established for leaders of women's groups and production teams, and materials for their instruction were circulated in aid of their training.[2] During these courses women leaders were encouraged to regard their work among women as an independent contribution of great political significance for the fortunes of women and the country. They were expected to take the lead in entering social production and sharing in the work of the women's production groups. This provided an excellent means of learning about the conditions of the women workers and acquainting themselves with their opinions and problems. It would also give them the necessary knowledge to arrange work schedules, labour protection and represent the opinions of the women labourers within the collective.

(d)   Women were encouraged to enter into agricultural collectives in their own right as individual and equal partners with the men. Symbolic of their individual and equal status was the guiding principle of equal pay for equal work for both men and women. One article on the subject explained the implications of this slogan:

> Equal pay for equal work means that all labourers, whether they are men or women, are entitled to the same rating and the same remuneration when they have completed the same job of the same quality.[3]

Although in the early years of collectivisation the remuneration due to women was normally paid to the male head of the household, the establishment of the communes ruled that payments should be made directly to the women themselves. The benefits of directly and individually receiving payments for their own work was to be used as an incentive encouraging individual women to enter into social production. A measure of economic independence was not only a desirable end in itself, but it was deemed to be a means to furthering the individual prestige and authority of women within the household or the village. In one co-operative, the women's leader tried to persuade the women to work in the fields by explaining that only active work could liberate them. In response to the common reaction of the older women that they were too old and did not care whether they were emancipated or not, the leader made the benefits more personal. "Your husband looks down on you and you haven't any decent clothes. If you come out to the fields there'll be more earnings in the family and your husband will respect you.[4] The promise of more respect and authority from the men of the household and of the village once women became a visible economic asset and shared in their support was stressed as the largest benefit available to individual women.

---

[1] Editorial, RMRB, 8 March 1959; Report from a Jiangsu commune, Hongqi, 3 Mar. 1973..

[2] Teaching materials on duties relating to work with rural women, ZF, 1 Feb. 1962.

[3] "Equal pay for equal work", Qian Xian (front line), 25 May 1964.

[4] Shen Chilan: <u>Women of New China</u>, P's C, 16 Aug. 1953.

(e) An important measure designed to enable women to enter into
    social production with a "composed mind" was the establishment
    of collective or communal services to reduce the individual
    household responsibilities and chores which have long occupied
    women.[1] These activities were time-consuming and onerous in
    rural China where on top of the daily washing, cooking and
    child care, water had to be fetched and carried, grain had
    to be ground at a stone or turned by a donkey or by the house-
    wife herself, fuel had to be gathered from the hills, clothes
    and cloth shoes sewn by hand, and vegetables pickled or sliced
    and dried for the long winter months. The new policies
    recognised that under conditions like these most women would
    find it impossible to take part in regular social production.
    A spokesman for the Government pointed out at a conference in
    1958 that its main task was to remove the contradictions
    between social production and household labour and that this
    kind of contradiction could only be resolved if steps were
    taken to substitute the scattered household tasks by
    collectivising grain processing, child care and cooking,
    eating or dining facilities.[2] To this end the Government
    and the Women's Federation advocated the development of a
    network of community dining rooms, nurseries, kindergartens,
    grain processing plants, sewing and other centres to make
    "all-round arrangements for the people's livelihood". Those
    which already existed were to improve the quality of their
    services and expand their scope. The Executive Committee of
    the Women's Federation recommended that there should be no
    hard and fast rules governing the particular form of their
    development, rather "we should develop collective welfare
    and social services undertaking in diverse forms and at
    different scales and standards so as to meet as far as
    possible the needs of different persons, different seasons,
    different productive pursuits".[3] Under the auspices of the
    rural communes, domestic labour was thus to be gradually
    socialised in order to free women for social production.

(f) To enable women to take a full and wide-ranging part in social
    production, the Government and the women's movement intro-
    duced measures to protect the health of rural women. The
    Labour Insurance Law had already guaranteed working mothers
    56 days' maternity leave with full pay. A network of health
    clinics was to be set up within each collective to improve
    the hygiene of child birth and the health of mothers and
    infants during the pre- and post-natal periods. Women were
    to be given the freedom to plan and space their families to
    reduce the toll of constant child-bearing on women's health
    and physical strength. Clinics with specially trained
    personnel were to provide facilities for the requisite informa-
    tion and birth control supplies.

---

[1] "Further liberate women's labour capacity ...", RMRB,
2 June 1958; "Equal pay for equal work ...", Hongqi, 1 Mar. 1972.

[2] "A new contradiction has to be solved", RMRB, 13 July 1958.

[3] "Women's movement in China enters on new stage", NCNA,
24 Feb. 1960.

Within social production there was to be a constant adjust-
ment of work assignments to safeguard the health of each
woman. Because of physiological differences, women were
to be "properly looked after in the matter of labour allocation during menstruation, pregnancy, birth and lactation".[1]
During these four events it was stipulated that women's
labour should be adjusted in the following ways: during
menstruation women should not be assigned to work posts or
at the very least must be assigned to the dry fields and
not paddy fields; during pregnancy women were to be allocated
light but not heavy work and during lactation to a place
nearby and not far away. Women production team leaders were
required to particularly concern themselves with the welfare
of the women members of their teams.[2] They were to acquaint
themselves with the welfare of the women members, with the
general situation of the whole team and confer with the male
team leaders in the allocation of labour.

(g) The plans for the expansion of production deliberately created
a shortage of manpower which in itself demanded the immediate
substitution of man's labour power by an alternative and the
utilisation of women's labour power. The men were withdrawn
from the agricultural workforce on a temporary basis into
projects of capital construction, water conservancy and new
rural industries which left a shortage of labour in the
agricultural production groups.[3] This policy not only over-
came the problem of underemployment, but also insured a ready
supply of labour to priority projects and opened up
opportunities for the employment of women on the other. In
this way the women could directly see for themselves that
the subsistence of the collective was dependent on their
working, weeding, watering, harvesting and planting.[4] In
their own eyes and in the eyes of the men they would hence-
forth become a necessary and valued part of the labour force.

(h) Women were to be actively encouraged to acquire new skills
and techniques, and collectives were constantly reminded to
establish training classes to teach women the techniques of
ploughing, raking, seed mixing and manure application and to
include women in the agricultural groups sent away for training in tractor driving and maintenance and other skills.[5]
It was recommended in the mid-1950s that women should make up
at least 30 per cent of the training classes run by the county,
district or township.[6] Women were also encouraged to support
programmes for mechanisation and electrification which would
greatly eliminate or at least reduce the amount of toilsome
physical labour in agriculture and favour women's full
participation in agriculture.[7]

---

[1] "Further liberate women's labour capacity", RMRB, 2 June
1958.

[2] "Further improve the labour protection work for members of
rural communes", ZF, 1 Aug. 1961.

[3] KMRB, 21 Aug. 1958.

[4] NCNA, 24 Feb. 1959; PR, 10 Mar. 1961.

[5] NCNA, 24 Feb. 1959.

[6] See: Socialist upsurge in China, FLP, Peking, 1959, p. 279.

[7] Report by President of ACDWF, RMRB, 7 Oct. 1959.

One measure of the success of these mobilisation policies in rural China is the degree to which women have contributed to the total labour inputs in collective units.   This can be assessed both according to the numbers of women who have entered social production and the proportion of labour time reckoned in numbers of actual days which have been worked by women.

Women in production

The first concerted effort by the Communist Party to mobilise women to enter social production had occurred in the northern provinces in the bases governed by the Communists in the 1940s during the anti-Japanese War.   At this time the men were recruited into the armies and women were encouraged to take up agricultural pursuits and sideline occupations such as spinning and weaving. In 1949 it was estimated that an average of 40 to 50 per cent of all able-bodied women took part in agriculture in these Soviet bases.   This figure was known to have reached as high as 70. to 90 per cent in some areas.[1]   By 1950 and at the time new measures were introduced on a nationwide basis to encourage rural women into social production this figure for the old liberated areas in the north had averaged out to between 50 and 70 per cent[2] compared to the figure of 20 to 40 per cent in the newly liberated areas in central and south China.[3]   There are no further figures available until the first stages of collectivisation in the mid-1950s. Before this period there is no reason to believe that land reform had especially contributed to an increase in the numbers of women entering social production.   Women were allotted their share of the land, but because of the patriarchal relations within the household and the inexperience of women in labouring and field management it seems more likely that the redistribution of land strengthened the resources of the household head rather than benefited and encouraged individual women to take up production.[4]

In quantitative terms the greatest increase in women's contribution to total labour inputs came with the establishment of collectives.

The establishment of co-operatives providing for an expansion in agriculture and the scope of occupations was responsible for the first sharp rise in number of women entering social production. It was estimated that the first stage of co-operativisation in 1956-57 had increased by six times the contribution of women to social production compared to that of 1955.[5]

---

[1] Documents of the women's movement in China, Peking, 1969, p. 30.

[2] "Chinese women help build new China", P's C., 16 Mar. 1950.

[3] "Historic change of several hundred million rural women ...", NCNA, 22 Sept. 1959.

[4] E. Croll: "The negotiation of marriage in the PRC", Ph.D. thesis, University of London, 1978, pp. 250-52.

[5] "Women's congress and education in socialism", NCNA, 29 Aug. 1957.

Table 2: Percentage of women in social production in rural
          China in the 1950s

Area	Date	Numbers of women (percentage of working age women, 16-60)
Old liberated areas) New liberated areas)	1950	50-70% (i) 24-40% (ii)
Rural China	1957	60-70% (ii)
Rural China	1958	90% (iii)

Sources: (i) P's C,16 Mar. 1950
           (ii) NCNA, 22 Sept. 1959
          (iii) NCNA, 31 July 1958

The number of women in social production was thought to be
roughly 100 million out of a total of 157 millions of working age
women or 60 per cent of their number.[1] During busy seasons this
number was reported to have risen to 70 per cent.[2] A number of
individual surveys also indicate an increase in both the numbers
of women entering agriculture and the average number of days
worked by female labourers in collective projects. One of these
surveys of 29 higher-stage co-operatives in Chekiang Province in
1956 shows the increase in labour days contributed by co-operative
members compared to those common on individual farms, mutual aid
teams and lower-stage co-operatives.

Table 3: Changes in labour utilisation rates

Labour type	No. of persons	Work days	PERCENTAGE INCREASE COMPARED TO THE DAYS OF -		
			Individual farming	Mutual aid teams	Lower-stage agricultural co-operatives
Male full-time labour	267	259	50	24.5	9.8
Male part-time labour	42	197	112	72.0	41.7
Female full-time labour	132	162	184	85.2	42.1
Female part-time labour	95	75	650	29.7	41.5

Source: Chao Kuo-chan, Agrarian policy of the Communist Party,
          1921-59, pp. 261-2.

[1] "Chinese women", CNA, 7 Feb. 1958.

[2] "Historic change of several hundred million rural women ...",
NCNA, 22 Sep. 1959.

Another survey shows the increase in the average number of days worked by each female labourer in collective projects from 1955 (lower-stage co-operatives) to 1957 (higher-stage co-operatives). Although women did not join the collective labour force in the same proportions as men, they did increase their share of work days during the years.

Table 4: Proportion of male and female labour units and average number of labour days for male and female labour units, 1955, 1957

	TOTAL 1955	1957	MALE 1955	1957	FEMALE 1955	1957
Share of labour units	100.0	100.0	54.8	56.7	45.2	43.3[1]
Share of labour days[2]	100.0	100.0	75.6	71.7	23.5	28.5
Average number of labour days per labour unit	96	175	134	204	50	105

[1] This small decline may be the result of an increase in male labour participation in collective work which disguises a simultaneous increase in female participation.

[2] What is important is the increase in the average number of labour days within male and female labour categories, for a "labour day" does not equal a full day's work; it is a conceptual tool based on a day's labour by a skilled man. Women may work a full day and still only earn the equivalent of three-fifths of a labour day.

Source: J. Salaff: "Institutionalised motivation for fertility limitation" in M. Young's Women in China: Studies in social change and feminism, Michigan Reports in Chinese Studies, No. 15, University of Michigan, 1973, pp. 94-144.

In the mid-1950s women still tended to work fewer actual days of work than men. The following data for 1957 shows that women are concentrated in those classes of workers who contribute fewer work days. Almost two-thirds of the women worked less than 100 days a year.

Table 5: Days worked by male and female workers in 228 agricultural producers' co-operatives, 1957

Number of days worked per year	All labour units	Male labour units	Female labour units
0-50	17.6	6.5	32.2
51-100	19.6	11.9	29.7
101-150	18.6	18.3	19.0
151-200	18.3	24.0	10.9
201-365	25.9	39.3	8.2
Total	100.0	100.0	100.0

Source: P. Schram: The development of Chinese agriculture, 1950-59, p. 163.

The same survey revealed continuing regional differences in female labour force participation. Women still work almost twice the number of labour days in the southern rice regions where there is double rice cropping and winter wheat as in other areas. Where there is only one major crop, as in the wheat areas of the north which are tilled by plough, fewer women contribute to agricultural production.

Table 6: Women's contribution to production by main geographical area, 1957

Area (district)	Percentage of total labour force		Average number of days worked		Percentage of total working days	
	Male	Female	Male	Female	Male	Female
NW and inner Mongolian	60.1	39.9	170	88	74.5	25.5
North-east	65.3	34.7	185	60	85.5	14.5
Central	55.8	44.2	195	84	74.6	25.4
Southern	54.3	45.7	226	133	66.8	33.2

Source: Joint Publications Research Service (JPRS), Washington, 41, 914, p. 5.

The peak of the campaigns to encourage women to enter social production occurred in 1958-59 during the period of the Great Leap Forward and the establishment of the communes. The new opportunities for women's labour participation afforded by the establishment of communes was drawn out in one commentary:

> The former agricultural producers' co-operatives were generally rather small scale and managed only agriculture and some small-scale secondary productive undertakings. Thus there was a certain limit to the possibility of fully absorbing women to perform productive labour and of providing reasonable arrangements for them to take part in production according to the specific attributes of women. People's communes, characterised by their larger size and public ownership are capable of conducting large-scale projects for building agriculture and water conservancy projects, developing diversified management of agriculture, forestry, stock breeding, fishing and secondary productive undertakings and gradually promoting the simultaneous development of industry and agriculture. All these created the favourable conditions for extensive participation in the performance of labour by women.[1]

The peak demand for women's labour during this period was the result of the expansion in the scope of activities managed by the communes and the removal of men into projects of water conservancy, irrigation and capital construction sponsored by the communes which created a shortage of labour within the smaller agricultural brigades or teams. Most of the reports published during the Great Leap Forward suggest that 90 per cent of the working age women in rural areas worked in social production during this period.[2]   This number included the large numbers of women recruited into the rural welfare services such as crèches and nurseries, sewing centres and community dining rooms which were established in large numbers during this particular period. Unfortunately this figure is nowhere broken down in any detail to indicate the number of actual working and labour days contributed by women. Although one report suggested that the average daily attendance of women in 1958 was 166 days and that this rose to 250 days in 1959, the second year of the Great Leap Forward.[3]   Another report suggests that women worked an average of 35 per cent of the total number of work days.[4]   This suggests a rise compared to the average of 24.6 per cent of the total working days given in table 5 for 1957.   In 1959 it was also estimated that women formed 45 per cent of the workforce[5] which compares with 45.2 and 43.3 per cent in 1955 and 1957 (see table 4).   Yet these over-all figures must be assumed to mask great variations within rural China.   In

---

[1] "The people's communes and women ...", NCNA, 29 Feb. 1960.

[2] Report by President of ACDWF, RMRB, 7 Oct. 1959;   NCNA, 1 Mar. 1960.

[3] "The people's commune and women", Hongqi, 29 Feb. 1960.

[4] "Women in China", CNA, 25 Mar. 1960.

[5] "Chinese women at work", PR, 10 Mar. 1961.

one detailed study of a commune which is available there was a
marked variation even within the commune itself. In one brigade,
796 out of 823 able-bodied women were doing farm work fairly
regularly, but this was proportionately almost 50 per cent more
than in a neighbouring production brigade.[1]

In the 1960s and 1970s there are piecemeal reports as to the
levels of participation of women in social production and several
of these suggest that women were not always fully involved in it
and certainly not to the extent suggested by the figures for the
late fifties. Many refer to local campaigns which were held
periodically to increase the participation of women. Again there
seem to be regional variations with a higher proportion of women
labouring in the south. One report from the southern rice
provinces in 1965 records that women accounted for 54.3 per cent
of the total membership and their labour makes up 55.4 per cent
of the total labour input.[2] In one newspaper in the north of
China in the same year there was a reference to the problem that
women have not yet been fully mobilised to take part in collective
labour.[3] In another account from the north of China in 1969 it
is reported that many women did not take part in rural labour
before the establishment of the revolutionary committees during
the Cultural Revolution and even then some women remained at home,
perhaps performing a few odd jobs but certainly showing no wish
to labour on a regular basis throughout the year.[4] Several reports
in the 1970s continue to speak of low levels of participation before
describing the subsequent rise in the contribution of women following a campaign. In one county in northern Fujian (a southern
province) it was reported that rural women there took little part
in farm labour before a new movement in 1972 to mobilise and
organise women to participate in agricultural work. For example,
in one brigade only 35-36 of the 102 women who were capable of
labour had undertaken farm work on a regular basis.[5] It is not
easy to interpret the piecemeal reports and even allowing for a
certain amount of exaggeration of past shortcomings to highlight
contemporary successes there seems to be little doubt that although
there has been an over-all rise in the number of women taking part
in social production since the early fifties, there has been some
fluctuation in the numbers of women contributing labour at any one
time in the collectives. Set against the sharp increase in the
participation rates in the late fifties, for example, some allowance must be made for the subsequent reduction in the numbers who
laboured in the collectives during the 1960s and 1970s.

------

[1] I. and D. Crooks: The first years of Yangyi commune,
London, 1966, p. 247.

[2] Report Guangdong Province Women's Federation, ZF,
1 Aug. 1965.

[3] Report by Wang Yufeng, ZF, 1 Oct. 1965.

[4] "Rural women constitute a tremendous revolutionary force",
Hongqi, 30 Sep. 1969.

[5] "Equal pay for equal work in Fujian Xian", RMRB,
13 May 1973.

Over the past 25 years the female labour force has however increased substantially both in numbers entering social production and in the numbers of days worked.   But this over-all increase does mask a certain degree of fluctuation with many women entering and leaving the workforce according to local demand.   This may vary according to the different cropping regions in China and according to the range and diversity in economic pursuits or the degree to which a variety of non-agricultural activities supplement agricultural production.   Where there is intense agricultural cultivation or a wide variety of non-agricultural occupations, women have indeed entered social production in large numbers.   In all the aim of the systematic and comprehensive attempt to encourage the participation of women in agriculture was to provide conditions favourable to their entry into social production.   This it was assumed would alter the traditional sexual division of labour and re-allocate socio-economic resources in favour of women.

CHAPTER 3

The sexual division of labour

Within agricultural production the opportunities to undertake new pursuits have greatly expanded in scope over the past 25 years. As many commentaries on the division of labour have noted, women have moved from "an auxiliary to a main force within agriculture".[1] Underlying all the policies for training women has been a set of dual and conflicting assumptions: that women can perform exactly the same labour as men and that women have certain physical limitations which define the type of work in which they can labour. Each of these has affected the forms which the sexual division of labour have increasingly taken.

On the one hand policies subscribe to the commonly cited adage of Mao Tse-tung that "anything a man can do a women can also do".[2] On this basis women have been encouraged to enter into new occupations which were traditionally male preserves. There are now women tractor drivers, women fishing teams, women at the plough and women work teams who drain fields, build dams and plant forests where previously there were none. These groups are often referred to as March 8 (Women's Day) teams, women red flag holders, Iron Maiden's teams and consist in the main of younger and unmarried women of the collectives, that is those not involved in reproduction. Women have been trained in the new technologies of agricultural production such as large and hand tractor driving, mechanised transplanters and taught the skills of ploughing, raking, seed mixing and manure applications.[3] They have contributed to technical innovation themselves by improving certain types of tools such as wooden-track earth movers, and improved water wheel and a new hand cranking mill.[4] Women's experimental groups have received a share of scientific and technical inputs. On these plots they have been encouraged to experiment with new methods of cultivation, close planting, soil improvement, pest control, watering, manuring and seed mixing.[5] In 1958-59 it was estimated that approximately 13 million women took part in these scientific experiments. In Hubei Province 36 per cent of all women in the province cultivated 121,000 hectares of experimental land between them.[6] Very often the new methods were proved to be both feasible and successful and the results of the experimental groups have been popularised in the media for the past two decades.[7] Their entrance into former male preserves, technical and training programmes and scientific

---

[1] Report by the President of ACDWF, RMRB, 7 Oct. 1959.

[2] "Work hard to train women cadres", Hongqi, 1 Dec. 1973.

[3] "Women's new life in rural people's communes", NCNA, 24 Feb. 1959.

[4] "Historic change of several hundred million women ...", NCNA, 22 Sep. 1959.

[5] NCNA, 7 Mar. 1959; 6 Mar. 1967.

[6] "Chinese women's achievements in 1958", NCNA, 4 Jan. 1959.

[7] PR, 12 July 1960; RMRB, 14 Apr. 1975; NCNA, 4 Mar. 1976.

experiments have all served to increase their confidence and prove
the ability of women agricultural workers, but at the same time the
majority of women are still to be found in certain of the less-
skilled and lighter of the agricultural tasks as a result of the
second assumption also underlying the division of labour - that
women have certain physical limitations.

Certain types of work are believed to be more suited to women
than to men because of the nature of their physique, degree of
physical strength and physical characteristics. As one policy
statement pointed out:

> Physically some people are stronger while others are weak,
> some heavy manual farm jobs fit the stronger sex better.
> This is a division of labour based on physiological features
> of both sexes, and is appropriate. We can't impose the same
> framework on female and male commune members alike in disregard
> of the former's physiological features and physical power.
> In some kinds of work, women are less capable than men, but
> in others, they are better.[1]

Women are generally to be found tending to livestock such as pigs,
poultry, breeding silk worms, manure collection work, hoeing and
transplanting and they have taken a greater part in the production
of certain crops such as tea, cotton and rice rather than others.
These all have been traditionally associated with women's labour
albeit within the domestic rather than the collective sphere of
production.

Two examples of the division of labour in different communes
and 25 years apart gives some indication of the allocation of work
tasks in these particular communes.

Figure (a): Division of labour on commune
(rice, corn, sweet potatoes, wheat), 1956

Men	Women
Heavy work (ploughing, carrying heavy loads)	Lighter work
Irrigation, fostering well-grown seedlings	Preparing ash compost
Tilling rape fields	Harvesting rape
Subsidiary occupations	Growing early crops

Source: See Socialist upsurge in China's countryside, FLP, Peking, 1957, 289.

---

[1] "Equal pay for equal work for men and women", Hongqi,
1 Feb. 1972.

Figure (b): Division of labour on commune
(double rice cropping, winter wheat), 1977

Men	Women
Ploughing with water buffalo	Sowing seed
Carrying water	Transplanting rice seedlings
Driving tractors	Harvesting
Driving hand tractors	Carrying manure to the fields
Rural industries	Raising collective pigs

Source: E. Croll: "Chiang village: A household survey", CQ,
Dec. 1977, p. 805.

There is a tendency for women to be found in the lighter tasks
and this has had the effect of underlining and strengthening the
notion of a natural division of labour within agriculture between
heavy and light work on the one hand and skilled and unskilled
labour on the other. The reports in the media would suggest that
there is also a correlation between the division of labour within
agriculture and the demand for men to take part in non-agricultural
pursuits. That is where the opportunities afforded by the establishment of rural industry, projects of capital construction and
the sideline occupations of fishing, mining and forestry draw men
from the agricultural workforce, then a new division of labour has
grown up not within agriculture, indeed women may have had to take
up numerous new tasks hitherto performed by men, but between
agriculture and non-agricultural pursuits. The peak demand for
women's labour in 1958-59 was the result of the strategy to create
a shortage of labour by withdrawing men from agriculture, and this
pattern may have set a precedent which has become something of a
permanent feature of rural China. The first indication that this
might be so came in a document of 1958 which suggested that

> women will gradually replace men in all work suitable to women
> so as to bring about a reasonable rearrangement of the social
> labour force.[1]

The result of this policy is that in some areas women have
become the mainstay of farming work in the fields.

> Women should shoulder agricultural production. Men's labour
> power is needed to open mines, expand machine building
> industry, power plants, cement plants. These all call for
> new labour inputs. Generally speaking, these departments of
> industry employ mainly men labourers and provide only a few
> types of work that can be undertaken by women workers. Thus,
> up to a certain stage in the development of socialist con-
> struction, agricultural production will have to be undertaken
> mainly by women. Of course with the process of agricultural
> production mechanised and electrified agricultural production

---

[1] Report on Women's Conference by Tsai Chang, NCNA, 4 Dec. 1958.

will follow the pattern of industrial production. By that
time women can completely shoulder the responsibility.[1]

In one commune in which I visited in 1977 a more detailed
survey of my own contributes to this impression. That is in
communes where there are a larger number of alternative occupations,
women outnumber men in agriculture. In the village surveyed the
majority of the workforce (numbering 79 persons) was employed in
the production team although a number of men worked in non-
agricultural occupations. These were mainly to be found in the
small machinery factories, the coal mine or services run by the
commune, the county or the State.

Table 7: Occupations of working residents,
          Jiang village, Guangdong Province

Work	Men	Women	Total
Agricultural production team	26	38	64
Other occupations outside team	13	1	14
Barefoot doctor	1	-	1
Total	40	39	79

Source: E. Croll: Chiang village: A household survey, CQ,
         Dec. 1977.

What is particularly noticeable in the production team is that
women outnumber men and that all the women in the workforce, except
one, worked in the production team in agriculture. This was seen
to be an unsatisfactory division of labour and as such was receiving
some attention from the commune leaders. However, this division
of labour between agricultural and non-agricultural pursuits may be
a phenomenon particularly associated with the more urbanised and
industrial regions of the south, and northern and eastern coastal
provinces, and less with the central and more inland rural areas.
Although the references to this new division of labour in the media
and policy documents suggest that it may be a widespread phenomenon
in the former regions.

Throughout China women have entered into new activities, have
received a share of inputs and acquired new skills, but it is also
true to say that they are predominantly to be found in certain of
the less-skilled occupations to do with livestock and particular
crops. The evidence also suggests that where there is a demand
for men's labour outside of agriculture, there may have been a
degree of feminisation of agriculture thus setting up a new sexual
division of labour between agricultural and non-agricultural
pursuits. These divisions of labour both within agriculture and
between agricultural and other activities have affected the rates
of remuneration due to women.

[1] NCNA, 1 Jan. 1959.

The remuneration of women

One of the main changes within the rural social field which has directly affected women is that they now receive individual remuneration for work performed within the collective. Since the establishment of rural communes, wages in kind and cash have been paid to them as individual workers rather than to the heads of households as previously. The separation of collective production from the domestic domain and the direct involvement of women in social production have allowed for the visibility and recognition of women as producers. There has also been a consistent forwarding of the policy of equal pay for equal work and some women have been remunerated on the same basis as the male labourers within the collective. Often they have only received equal payment after challenging the men to a competition in which they proved themselves equal to the men in performance, or the men themselves when challenged fail to equal women in the performance of women's allocated tasks. Cases of the reassessment of remuneration to equalise the payments made to men have been constantly cited in the media,[1] but equal pay is still not a constant feature in the rural collective.

Labour in the collective sector is rewarded according to the system of work points or labour days. Agricultural tasks of individual workers are evaluated according to the degree of strength, skill and experience required, quantity and quality of output and then norms are set for the standards and pace of each type of work or worker and a value assigned to the labour day. Ten work points generally equalled one labour day but all workers labouring a full day do not necessarily receive ten work points. The number of work points were designed to reward skill and physically hard work and on both these counts women or the jobs assigned to women normally received a low estimation. Whereas men were often assigned ten work points for a day's work, women almost always automatically received less whether they were labouring at the same or different tasks. Where individual workers were themselves graded, and for each full day's work allotted a specific number of work points usually ranging from four to ten points (seven grades), women tended to be distributed among the lowest of the three payment grades (see table 8).

In the preferred method of remuneration, work points are awarded differentially to agricultural tasks, women also perpetually receive a lower number of work points than men. Table 9 suggests a certain discrepancy which has persisted over the years in the number of work points paid to men and women.

This discrimination has been a major factor affecting the morale of women in the collectives, and several reports in the media describe situations where women had withdrawn their labour or made only half-hearted attempts to maintain their quotas and subsequent investigation found the cause to lie in their

---

[1] "Shen Chilan - women of new China", P's C, 16 Aug. 1953; report from Yingshan Xian, ZF, 1 Nov. 1961; "Equal pay for equal work for men and women", Hongqi, 1 Mar. 1972.

Table 8: Distribution of the 1,453 male and female
          agricultural workers by wage grades, Sun Fen
          Production Brigade, Kungming People's
          Commune, 1958

Wage grade	Distribution in each grade			Proportion in each grade	
	Total	Men	Women	Men	Women
1	12.4	5.8	18.4	22.2	77.8
2	16.0	12.7	18.9	38.0	62.0
3	26.4	21.2	31.2	38.3	61.7
4	23.4	23.1	23.7	47.0	53.0
5	9.5	14.1	5.3	71.0	29.0
6	7.5	13.4	2.1	85.3	14.7
7	4.8	9.7	0.4	95.7	4.3
	100.0	100.0	100.0		

Source: Extract from China mainland magazines, 164, 13 Apr.
         1959; C. Hoffman: Work incentive practices and
         policies in the PRC, 1953-1965, NY, 1967, p. 319.

Table 9: Allocation of work points to male and
          female labourers per day, random
          sample, 1956-1975

Date	Men	Women	Source
1956	10	4-6	FLP, 1957, 289
1960	10-12	8	Crooks, 1966, p. 126
1961	10	7	ZF, 1 Nov. 1961
1961	10	8	ibid.
1964	6-10	less than 5.5	Qian Xian, 25 May 1964
1965	10	7.5	ZF, 1 Feb. 1966
1970	10	5	RMRB, 6 Mar. 1972
1972	10	8	Hongqi, 1 Feb. 1972
1975	10	7	CR, June 1975
1975	10	7.5	CR, Mar. 1975

dissatisfaction with the inadequacy of their rewards.[1]   Despite
the consistent advocacy of the principle and numerous campaigns to
implement it, there has been a tenacious opposition to allocating
women remuneration equal with that of the men.   There have been a
number of rationalisations put forward to justify the continuing
discrepancy in payments and lower evaluation of their jobs which
after all lies at the heart of the problem.

        (a) It is claimed that women do not yet bear the main brunt
of agricultural work for men still do the heavier and more basic
work in the collectives.[2]   Even in the instances where women
perform the same tasks as men, these are deemed to be the exceptions
to the rule that women just do not match the stronger capacity for
labour of men and their higher technical levels.[3]   Therefore,
until women learn to do exactly the same kinds of jobs as men they
do not deserve equal payment.[4]   It is in connection with this
claim that we find the policy of labour protection being used to
justify the weaker physical capacity of women and the lower evaluation of their jobs.   In these cases the criteria for assessment is
dominated by physical strength instead of also including quality and
quantity and attitude towards work.

        (b) Men have argued that their positions as heads of households
means that they must be the main breadwinners or contributors to
the household budget.   They were reluctant to allow women and
especially their daughters whose earnings would be lost to the
household on marriage to be the main contributors to the budget.[5]

        (c) One repercussion of equal pay that was openly feared was
the likely diminishing value of the work point should women be
allowed to earn more than the upper limits set by the collective.
After each harvest the value of the work point was calculated by
dividing the total number of work points earned by all the members
of the collective into that portion of the total income of the
collective set aside for individual earnings.   What was feared was
that if women received a higher rating for their work, the total
number of work points would rise and by making no allowance for a
concomitant increase in total output it seemed as if the value of
each work point would fall.[6]   This the men thought would affect
their own levels of payment.

        (d) Women did not deserve equal payment for the tasks they
performed for they did not work the same time as men.   Women had
household tasks and responsibilities which meant they were unable

----

        [1] P's C, 16 July 1957; ZF, 1 Nov. 1961; Qian Xian, 25 May
1964; ZF, 1 Oct. 1965; Hongqi, 1 Mar. 1972.

        [2] "Li Fang - people's deputy", P's C, 1 Jan. 1954.

        [3] Qian Xian, 25 May 1964; I. and D. Crooks, 1966, pp. 126-29.

        [4] ZF, 1 Nov. 1961; CR, Mar. 1975.

        [5] I. and D. Crooks, 1966, pp. 126-29.

        [6] I. and D. Crooks, 1966, pp. 126-29; PR, 11 Mar. 1966;
Hongqi, 1 Mar. 1972.

to give the same number of work days as men.   Since each household consists of both men and women, no single household will suffer economic loss.[1]

(e) Lastly, the importance of the problem was generally under-stated and misrepresented as one of merely adjusting women's remuneration by a few work points[2] rather than one which was crucial for the entrance and maintenance of women's labour input and symbolic of the value placed on women's labour and contribution to rural development as a whole.

Reproduction and household services

At the same time as the Government encouraged women to enter social production it also demanded that the collectives accommodate and cater for women's reproductive capacity and reduce the demands of the household on their labour.   Over the years women have increasingly benefited from the measures taken to improve and protect the health of rural women.   At first when women initially entered production in large numbers there were several reports which commented on the numbers of miscarriages and other casualties due to overstrain and insufficient care and protection.[3]   The national women's organisations undertook to report the matter to the central Government and circulated to its members memoranda on the problem.[4] Since this time members of the communes have implemented labour protection policies and women tended to either work fewer days per month or be allocated to dry and light work for fewer hours when they were menstruating, were pregnant or during the period following childbirth.   However, it has also been necessary for policy documents on labour protection to continue to remind collectives of the importance of these measures for the health and productivity of women.[5]   They blamed both the leaders of the collectives for giving the problem insufficient attention and women themselves for dis-regarding their health and indulging in simplistic physical contests.[6] Apparently some women continued to feel that the labour protection policies reflected the delicacy of women and hesitated to inform their leaders when they were menstruating and pregnant and in special need of safeguarding their health.

From the early 1950s onwards the Government and the women's movement had paid attention to improving hygiene and methods of childbirth and the health of mothers and infants during the pre- and post-natal periods.   By 1956 it was estimated that trained

[1] ibid.

[2] ibid., "Equal pay for equal work", Hongqi, 6 Mar. 1972.

[3] "The health of rural women", RMRB, 16 May 1956;   ibid., 12 Aug. 1956.

[4] "Forum of non-party women", NCNA, 6 June 1957.

[5] "Further liberate women's labour capacity ...", RMRB, 2 June 1958;   "Bring into fuller play women as members of the labour force", Hongqi, 3 Mar. 1973.

[6] "Further improve the labour protection work ...", ZF, 1 Aug. 1961.

health workers supervised 60 per cent of rural births thus greatly
reducing infant and maternal mortality.[1]   Before the movement to
train barefoot doctors and establish a widespread network of local
clinics in each production brigade in the mid-1960s, the rural
areas had tended to be medically understaffed.   The training of
para-medical personnel and the practice of assigning a women
barefoot doctor to each production brigade who both worked alongside
the women members in production and spread health knowledge
generally served to keep a health check and treat women workers.
The Government has established a network of local clinics which have
systematised the health services in rural areas and provided
facilities for birth control, the treatment of elementary problems
with herbs and acupuncture and referrals of the most serious cases
to the commune hospital.   Indeed these facilities have been the
envy of many international health and planned parenthood bodies.

The separation of the public and domestic spheres underlay the
traditional division of labour and their merger was crucial to its
alteration.   Articles in the media over the years have made it
clear that what is to be avoided in the process of rural development
if the entry of women into the public sphere with the result that
they merely acquire dual roles with ensuing conflict or physical
strain, or alternatively, that women's domestic roles prevent them
from fully participating in political processes many of which in the
rural villages are spare time and unpaid.   Thus, the Government has
also demanded of the collectives that they establish a number of
community services such as crèches, nurseries, grain grinding,
sewing centres and dining facilities to reduce the household
responsibilities and chores of individual women.   It was not until
the late 1950s that there was a concerted effort during the Great
Leap Forward to establish a number of collective services to
socialise household labour such as rearing children, processing
food grain, preparing meals and sewing clothes.   During this
period the majority of production brigades could boast a range of
services available to women.   By 1959 it was estimated that in
rural areas there were 4,980,000 nurseries and kindergartens and
more than 3,600,000 public dining rooms.[2]   The advantages for
women were stressed and applauded.   One collective calculated that
whereas 105 persons were required for preparing meals for 105
households in the past, now 8 persons were sufficient thereby making
it possible to save over 6,000 labour days for the whole year.
According to another survey in Honan, employment of sewing machines
and hand-operated mills alone helped to cut down women's household
labour by 40 to 50 per cent.[3]

The establishment of these collective living enterprises was
heralded as resolving the age-old contradiction between participation
by women in social production and the demands of the household on
their labour.   However, although an impressive array of these
services was established in the late 1950s, some were shortly
afterwards closed as suddenly as they had been opened.   Child care

---

[1] J. Salaff: "The role of the family in health care" in
J.R. Quin (ed.), Medicine and health care in China, US Dept. of
Health, 1972, p. 34.

[2] Editorial, RMRB, 8 Mar. 1959.

[3] "Further liberate women's labour capacity ...", RMRB,
2 June 1958.

facilities were closed due to a shortage of trained personnel, a dissatisfaction with the level of care and the widespread availability of grandmothers to look after the children. The establishment of community dining rooms in rural areas proved to be very expensive as formerly unpaid domestic labour became paid labour in the public sector. The wages of the cooks now had to be paid. Whereas members of individual households had formerly gathered fuel for their stoves from the surrounding hillsides, now coal was required, it had to be purchased from the commune station and the collective cart had to be spared to transport it. Popular opinion and dissatisfaction with the organisation of menus and accounting often led to their closure. Certain pragmatic factors also militated against their successful maintenance. For instance, in northern China it was still necessary to light individual stoves for heating purposes, and since it was the lighting and permanent use of the stoves which took most of the time and effort of individual women, the establishment of communal dining rooms had only a peripheral impact on reducing domestic labour. As a result of a combination of factors the community dining rooms closed.[1] Perhaps the most successful of the services established were the communal corn-grinding facilities many of which have remained in operation.

Since this large-scale experiment in establishing rural welfare facilities in the late 1950s, community services have been very unevenly established in rural areas. In the 1970s nurseries and early child care are provided on some of the largest and well-to-do communes located on the outskirts of the urban centres. It is my own observation and that of others that nurseries are usually for children of 3 years and upwards and they are by no means universally established in rural villages. Some collectives organise rudimentary child-minding services during harvesting and sowing. At other times arrangements are made between the women within individual households and grandmothers often retire to mind grandchildren. Ruth Sidal was told that even in communes with many regular nurseries, half, or more than half, of the children stay with grandmothers.[2] Where young mothers can make no such arrangements and there is no child-care facilities they usually have to withdraw from the collective labour force. For instance, it has been reported that "few mothers with children have the opportunity to work in the fields".[3] Most of the community dining rooms did not survive the Great Leap Forward. Although in very busy agricultural seasons canteens might be set up by the collective to reduce the labour required by individual households.

Since the end of the Great Leap Forward policy statements to do with the sexual division of labour within the household have been marked by a certain change over the past 15 years. At first women in the countryside were exhorted to take part in collective production as well as to maintain the household.[4] Later at the end of the 1960s and in the early 1970s men and women were encouraged to

---

[1] I. and D. Crooks, 1966, pp. 68-71, 157-58.

[2] R. Sidal: Women and child care in China, Penguin, 1972: 84-85, 124-25.

[3] J. Myrdal and G. Kessle: China: The Revolution continued, Penguin, 1973: 239.

[4] Reports of the Third Guangdong Provincial Women's Congress, Nanfang Ribao, 27 Mar. 1962.

undertake an equal share of the housework.[1]   If women were to move
into the collective sphere surely the corollary was that men should
move into the domestic sphere.   In the rural villages, meetings
have been held to encourage men to undertake their share.   This
policy may have had some results among the younger generation, but
even in the 1970s policy statements are marked by a certain
ambiguity.   As one article stated:

> Domestic work should be shared by men and women.   But some
> household chores, such as looking after children, sewing and
> others should generally be done by women ... after a certain
> phase of farm work is completed during very busy seasons or on
> rainy days or in winter, women should be given some time off
> to attend to some essential household chores.[2]

In 1974 articles in the media admitted that the question of
domestic labour is a continuing problem both because of limited
material conditions and the provision of services and the persisting
influence of male supremacy.[3]   In these conditions women continue
to maintain and service the household.   Without the outside agencies
to perform household work and to provide labour-saving devices which
are available to the urban housewife, rural women must continue to
transform most of what the household consumes.   Meat and vegetables
must be produced and cooked, food salted and preserved, children
cared for and the majority of clothes and shoes sewn.   Women within
the household usually divide these tasks between themselves, with
older women often retiring from collective labour to perform the
domestic tasks and care for young children.   There may be some
sharing between households during busy agricultural seasons, but in
rural China women still tend to perform the essential task of
maintaining and rearing workers for production.   The drawing of
women into social production and the reduction in the old sexual
division of labour between the public and domestic spheres then
juxtaposes a new division of labour in which women's unpaid labour
is distributed in favour of the domestic sphere to the detriment of
their participation in political decision making.

Political status

It had been forecast that one of the benefits accruing to
women as a result of entry into social production would be access
to and a share in the control and allocation of the resources of
the household and the collective.   Within the household the status
of individual women seems to have improved as a result of their
visible contributions to the family budget.   In several life
histories women report that the attitude of their husband and
mother-in-law altered once they began to earn wages for their work.
But although girls and women have become potential and actual wage-
earning contributors to the household budget, the fact that they
generally earn less than their male counterparts and that their
earnings are lost by their natal household on marriage means that
there is still a marked preference for the birth of sons.

---

[1] "Work hard to train women cadres", Hongqi, 1 Dec. 1973.

[2] "Bring into fuller play the role of women as labour force",
Hongqi, 3 Mar. 1973.

[3] "Work hard to train women cadres", Hongqi, 1 Dec. 1973.

As they laboured in the collectives so they would begin to
share in the decision making of the collective and hence enter the
local and national public and political domain.   One measure of
female power can be taken to be the number of women cadres or
women who are in positions of responsibility in the Communist
Party, government organs and production units.   These figures
indicate that the expansion in the numbers of women entering social
production was not reflected in the numbers of women admitted to
party membership or selected for positions of decision making in
the high level or government organs.   To take the membership of
the Communist Party and the Youth League as examples, women make
up only 10 per cent of the party membership, in the 1950s, 30 per
cent of the Young Communist League,[1] and of the basic-level
people's deputies elected in all parts of the country the proportion
of women rose very slowly.

Table 10:   The proportion of women among
            basic-level deputies

Date	Women	Men	Source
1953	17.3%	82.7%)	
1958	20.0%	80.0%)	NCNA, 22 Sep. 1959
1963	22.36%	77.64%	PR, 8 Jan. 1965

Despite a number of campaigns to encourage women to take part in
political decision-making bodies, their number remains dispropor-
tionately low in the 1970s.   True there has been an increase in
the numbers of women cadres since the Cultural Revolution.   Of the
6 million new members admitted to the Communist Party between 1966
and 1973, 27 per cent were reported to be women.[2]   In the provi-
sional congresses of the newly reconstituted Young Communist League
in 1973 an average of 40 to 45 per cent of the delegates were
women.[3]   In Honan Province, women accounted for 30 per cent of
cadres of the agricultural production brigades.[4]   Several newspaper
reports have commented on these figures and expressed some dissatisfaction at the continuing low proportions.[5]

Women have indeed shared in the establishment of a new development process in rural areas, and the very form which this development
process took has depended on women's participation in social production.   They have entered social production in large numbers to
the extent that in many areas they are now the main producers in
agriculture.   They now receive individual wages and their health
and levels of education and training in skills have improved

---

[1] J. Lewis: Leadership in Communist China, NY, 1963, p. 109.

[2] RMRB, 1 July 1973.

[3] J. Maloney: Current scene XII, 3-4, 1976.

[4] RMRB, 6 Mar. 1972.

[5] RMRB, 8 Mar. 1973.

substantially.   There have been continued attempts to reduce their
household responsibilities and to encourage them to participate in
the collective decision-making processes.   But many of these
benefits have not reached their full potential and some more than
others still fall far short of their stated goals.   By the early
1960s when all four legal, economic, ideological and organisational
strategies had been introduced and implemented, it was becoming
evident that certain obstacles were inhibiting the further redefinition of the position of women.   These various obstacles can be
categorised into three main problem areas to do with the relation of
social production to female status, the structure and function of
the rural household and the separation of women into female
solidarity groups.   Campaigns in the 1960s and 1970s have attempted
to clearly identify and resolve each of these problem areas.   The
following three chapters discuss each of these three main economic,
ideological and organisational constraints which continue to affect
the productive and reproductive roles and status of women in rural
areas.

CHAPTER 4

The intervention of ideological constraints

The close of the first decade of Communist government marked the end of a period in which the policies of the Government and the women's movement were based on the assertion that women were oppressed or subordinated mainly because they were cut off from socially productive labour. At the end of the first decade, both the Government and the women's movement were questioning the assumed correlation between social production and improvements in the position of women. Despite the widespread incorporation of Chinese women into social production, thus fulfilling one of the necessary conditions for change in female status the degree of change had been somewhat less than expected. Participation in social production might be a necessary condition for improving female status, but it was not a sufficient condition. The new policies of the 1960s reflected the growing belief in the People's Republic of China that it was ideological constraints, as opposed to material constraints, which primarily inhibit further changes in the position of women.

Indeed it was the very entry of women into the labour force on a wide scale in the Great Leap Forward in the late 1950s, and the attempted establishment of new social institutions designed to remove certain of the structural constraints, that were said to be responsible for highlighting the fundamental problem that confronted women - the removal of a whole history of cultural oppression or institutionalised or internalised subordination. Beliefs elaborated on women's supposed inferiority, self-abasement and dependence survived transformations in the mode of production. Experience had shown that changes in the economic base and the creation or adoption of new social institutions did not necessarily result in the creation or adoption of a new ideology. For instance, it was still widely believed that "a man travels everywhere while a woman is confined to the kitchen", "a woman with an education is without virtue", "just as a mare can't go into battle, a woman can't go into politics", "women know of nothing but household affairs", "a well sunk by a woman will not yield water and a boat rowed by a woman will capsize" and "a woman having a job is like flying a kite under a bed" or "chicken feathers flying to heaven". So long as women themselves believed that their primary raison d'être was to feed, nourish and care for their individual families, they would not take advantage of the new institutions created to share in the maintenance of the household. At the end of the Great Leap Forward an editorial in a national newspaper concluded that "only by enabling women to obtain their ideological emancipation will it be possible for them to develop their infinite source of power".[1] The women's movement came to the conclusion that as long as women did not recognise the continuing influence of the deep-rooted habits of the old ideology which still discriminated against and showed contempt for them, and while women themselves held traditional conceptions of the female role, it would not be possible for them to take advantage of the opportunities available to them in the new society.

---

[1] "Further liberate women's labour capacity", RMRB, 2 June 1958.

The women's movement turned its attention to abolishing the ideological constraints as the following passage from a policy document issued by the Peking Women's Federation makes clear in 1962.

Now that the broad masses of women have taken part in productive labour can one say that there is no more work to be carried out among women? No, on the contrary, the contents of woman work are now richer than before, and we are now required to carry out this work more penetratingly, carefully and solidly. For instance, though the broad masses of women have taken part in production, they still have many social problems in production, living and thought. The thought that women are inferior and dependent is present to a greater or lesser degree among the women themselves, and, in society the vestiges of feudal thought that women are contemptible cannot be thorough eliminated within a short time ... For this reason, it is not true to say that, there is not more work to be carried out among women, on the contrary the work in this respect must be reinforced.[1]

In order to arouse a common awareness of these problems, the women's movement embarked on what they called a "conscious learning process" in the 1960s to raise the consciousness of women to the ways in which the influence of the traditional ruling ideology continued to circumscribe their lives. "Without self-awareness", they said, "women will be unwilling to fly though the sky is high".[2] The consciousness-raising movement was organised on the twin premises that the continuing social secondariness of women had ideological foundations and that "first we women must begin with ourselves".[3] On the basis of the first premises many articles were published which couched the problem of redefining the position of women in ideological terms. That is the problem was wholly defined in terms of education in and accepting a new ideology incorporating a new role and status of women. For instance, the problem of combining the demands of production and reproduction[4] and the distribution of economic resources and rewards between men and women[5] could be overcome by simply identifying and then eliminating the continuing influence of old beliefs and attitudes. As a first step women were encouraged to start with themselves and articulate their individual experience and learn from each other in an "exchange of experiences" in their own local groups.

One article in the national Women's Magazine outlined what the process of consciousness raising should entail for local groups in the villages. In reply to the question "in what respects should we women be self-conscious?" it recommended that to bring the unconscious to the conscious, women's groups should meet and study their own individual life histories and the collective history of women, analyse the foundations of past subordination

---

[1] "Reference materials for training basic level cadres", ZF, 1 Feb. 1962.

[2] ZF, 1 Nov. 1960.

[3] "In what respects should women be self-conscious?", ZF, 1 Oct. 1963.

[4] "The relationship between work, children and household chores ...", ZF, 1 Nov. 1963.

[5] "Respect the opinions of women members on the question of payment", ZF, 1 Nov. 1961.

and compare it to their present and potential positions in society.
Such a self-examination, it suggested, would reveal the thought
patterns which governed the daily practice of their lives and the
continuing but often quite unconscious influences of beliefs such
as "the husband is responsible for supporting a family, while the
wife is responsible for household chores" or a "man is superior
to a woman", which underlay the sexual division of labour and the
evaluation of the sexes into superior and inferior categories.[1]
On these bases the necessity of reactivating women's local groups
was reiterated in the early sixties, and the national Women's
Federation sponsored a number of courses to train women representatives and women production team leaders in the new type of work.
They issued teaching materials for work among rural women which
emphasised that it was necessary at all times to go beyond the
abstract generalities and categoric statements and analyse the
practical problems and specific conditions of individual peasant
women.[2]

How far this movement to raise the consciousness of women was
effective is difficult to ascertain. It seems likely that in
many areas it merged into the Socialist Education Movement which
was a much broader movement to reduce the degree of conservative
thinking in the countryside. Whether or not it was extensive in
its influence, in the 1970s, a renewed emphasis on the ideological
aspects of the emancipation of women in the recent campaign to
criticise Confucius and Lin Piao (1973-74) affirms the belief that
it is the ideological constraints which 15 years later continue to
be identified as the primary obstacle preventing the full participation of women in the allocation of social and economic resources.
An editorial in the People's Daily published on the eve of the
recent campaign again emphasised that so far in China it had been
impossible to eliminate completely the remnants of Confucian
ideology advocating male supremacy and the division of labour into
the domestic and public spheres, and that the persistence of old
habits and customs underlying the discrimination against women in
the public sphere was a reflection of the influence of the traditional ruling ideology.[3] The campaign itself was described by
the women's organisation as "a deep socialist revolution in the
realm of ideology which was of great significance in the continuous
struggle to break down male supremacy and replace old habits and
customs".[4] Again it has been stressed that only if women are
determined to identify and criticise the influence of the ruling
ideology will they be able to "emancipate their minds, do away
with all fetishes and superstitions and press ahead despite the
difficulties".[5] Through a nationwide study programme the campaign

---

[1] "In what respects should women be self-conscious?", ZF,
1 Oct. 1963.

[2] "Reference materials for training basic level cadres", ZF,
1 Feb. 1962.

[3] Editorial, RMRB, 8 Mar. 1973.

[4] Foochow Radio, 7 Jan. 1974.

[5] "Smash the mental shackles that bind and enslave women",
RMRB, 2 Feb. 1974.

has aimed to identify and trace the origins and development of the
ideology responsible for the oppression of women and identify,
criticise and discredit the remaining influence and the traditional
ruling ideology.

For the first time women were widely encouraged to rediscover
and study their own history with a view to understanding the role
of the Confucian ideology, its origins, development and limitations
in determining the expectations and self-images of women. Numerous
study groups were formed some of which aimed to combine peasant,
worker and student women in the one group. Their historical
studies mainly aimed to draw attention to the "social origins and
class foundations" of the code of ethics which had so discriminated
against women. They stressed that male supremacy was neither an
immutable social principle ordained by heaven nor one dating back
to time immemorial, but was a principle developed by Confucius at
a specific historical period for a specific purpose. A few of
the groups have reported on their studies in the media, and their
writings have been widely circulated.[1] It was in criticising
Confucius that the women's groups said they had begun to realise
that the traditional division of labour and the evaluation of the
sexes into inferior and superior categories rested on social rather
than biological foundations. As one women's group concluded from
its studies, "the cruel oppression of women was not due to the
biological distinction between men and women, but was rooted in
the social system directed by a small handful of the exploiting
classes".[2] Women authors of an article on Confucian persecution
of women in history pointed out that it was only the identifica-
tion of the sources of oppression and widespread knowledge of the
social origins of male supremacy which allowed for the very
possibility of change.[3]

During the recent campaign, study groups have drawn attention
to the ways in which the traditional rules of propriety defined
and affected women's individual and personal life histories.
They studied the old written codes themselves and to demonstrate
their influence in practice, the older women were asked to tell
the stories of their lives in order that the younger women might
identify and analyse the precise influence of the Confucian code
of ethics on their lives. The Dajai Iron Women's Team reported
that through the study of women's histories "they were reminded
that the masses of working women were the most oppressed and
humiliated victims of the old ethical codes and their life
experiences served as a warning against the restoration of the
Confucian rites and rules of propriety".[4] In this way women's
groups began to document their own history. At the same time
the national media drew attention to the fact that their present

---

[1] e.g. KMRB, 14 Jan. 1974.

[2] ibid.

[3] Sun Loying and Lu Lifen: "On Confucian persecution of
women in history", Xuexi Yu Pipan, 10 Jan. 1975.

[4] "We revolutionary women bitterly hate the doctrines of
Confucius and Mencius", Hongqi, 3 Mar. 1974.

criticisms were part of a long tradition of resistance by women
to the influences of the ruling ideology. A group made up of
peasant women, women workers and students of history at Peking
Teachers' University suggested that far from being passive reci-
pients of ideological forces, women had participated in and even
led some of the movements for resistance against the Confucian
ruling ideology throughout the centuries of Imperial rule.[1]

The women's groups were encouraged to use this experience of
analysis in order to identify the remaining influence of the old
ideology on their lives today. In these same study groups women
were to identify the discrimination and prejudices which they
currently experienced and which shaped their own expectations of
themselves. Few women today had the ethical codes quoted to them
in their classical forms, but many peasant women could point to the
numerous folk sayings and proverbs which continued to operate
within their everyday experience to discourage women and belittle
their social contribution.[2] Under their influence young women
were said to still feel themselves to be less than equal with men.
To give peasant women more confidence the media has described how
many women have already broken ancient prohibitions and taboos and
entered into new occupations to do with agriculture and fishing
which were traditionally male preserves. An analysis of the
recent history of individual women and the women's movement in the
twentieth century was said to illustrate that change was possible
and proof that women have and should "smash the traditional myths
by their own action".[3] Over-all, the campaign has been planned on
the basis that only conscious knowledge can prevail against the
structures of subordination and there was therefore to be a determined effort to raise women's theoretical understanding of the role
of ideology in society.[4] Never again, it was emphasised, should
they allow men to monopolise and manipulate ideological resources
to the disadvantage of women.

The particular and practical aims outlined in the campaign
suggest that several problems in rural areas continue to concern
the Government and women's groups. These include the insufficient
representation of women in political and leadership positions,[5] the
problem of equal pay for women,[6] the persistence of traditional
marriage customs[7] and the division of labour within the household.[8]

---

[1] Theory group of People's Liberation Army, Report, RMRB,
8 Mar. 1975.

[2] The most common sayings disparage the leadership roles of
peasant women; it was like a donkey taking the place of a horse
which can only lead to trouble.

[3] KMRB, 6 Mar. 1974.

[4] Hongqi, 1 July, 1974, 3 Mar. 1974; NCNA, 7 Mar. 1975.

[5] ibid., 1 July 1974.

[6] RMRB, Nov. 1974.

[7] Xuexi Yu Pipan, 10 Jan. 1975; NCNA, 7 Mar. 1975.

[8] ibid., 10 Jan. 1975.

The campaign has identified the particular ideological constraints which continue to hinder the resolution of each of these problems. For each of these continuing problem areas, men and women's groups were reported in the media as coming to a new awareness of an old problem through the recognition of the ideological constraints originating in the Confucian principle of male supremacy. In the role models and reference groups portrayed in the media, the point at which change takes place coincides with the rejection of attitudes of conservatism and the acceptance of new norms. How far again the influence outlined in this study has permeated rural China must remain uncertain, but two things can be said:

(a) it forms one of the most concentrated and analytical attempts in China to date to integrate the redefinition of the female role with a nationwide effort to change the self images and expectations of both men and women; and

(b) the main interest of this campaign as far as the report is concerned lies in its confirmation that it is the ideological constraints, as opposed to the structural constraints, which are identified as primarily inhibiting the redefinition of the role and status of women.

The importance assigned to ideology in introducing and maintaining processes of social change and the emphasis placed on its communication reflects the quite central belief in the People's Republic of China that under certain circumstances ideology has its own power or to determine the base. That is ideology and organisation can serve as substitutes for the development of the material forces at least within certain limits, until conditions allow for further industrialisation and the development of the economic base. It is generally recognised that the uneven development of the urban and rural areas forms one of the greatest divisions in Chinese society in which the disparity between the two can and does work to the disadvantage of rural women. There is a tendency in China itself to interpret these differences in terms of the "backwardness" of rural women, or to look to the ideological origins of these disadvantages in that the countryside tends to form a repository of traditional and conservative custom and habit. However, it can be argued very cogently that in rural areas in China there are certain material restraints which also actively encourage the persistence of certain ideologies. This is not to argue that the ideological constraints are no less real or their removal pertinent to the solutions of continuing problems, but that it is structural constraints which equally or even more inhibit the further redefinition of the role and status of women in the rural social field.

CHAPTER 5

The rural household

In the rural areas of China there is some tension between the demands of a radical ideology and the demands of a harsh and often limiting economic base and it is the tension between the two which raises questions of importance for the position of women in conditions where the level of the productive forces may impose certain imperatives of its own on any strategies designed to redefine the position of women. It can be argued that in the countryside incomplete transformations in the mode of production encourage the persistence of certain of the ideological premises identified as restraints and that these have to do with the continuing exchange of women in marriage between patrilocal households and the functions of the latter in the rural economy. It is therefore to the structure and function of rural households that we must turn to identify and explain some of the variables which continue to ensure the social, economic and political secondariness of women in rural China.

In contemporary China the domestic group is defined as "mainly a unit of life in which the husband and wife share their married life together, rear and educate their children and care for their elder near relatives together".[1] This definition omits any reference to its property base or the socio-economic functions which have characterised the traditional domestic group in China and which underlie the usual anthropological definitions of the domestic group as "the residential unit, the unit of production, consumption and reproduction" in peasant societies. This is because in the 1950s a number of programmes were introduced into China to remove the property basis of the peasant household and to reduce their socio-economic functions as a unit of production. In the rural areas policies were implemented which gradually collectivised the land and collectively organised production and many subsidiary occupations. With the establishment of the communes, the production brigades and the production teams became the effective owners of the means of production and formed the basic units of accounting, planning and distribution of incomes. In both rural and urban areas it was anticipated that the establishment of collective consumer services such as common dining facilities, child care, laundry, food processing and other services would mean that a large part of consumption would not take place by and within the individual household.

Policies have also been introduced to reduce the influence of the individual household in attempting to control decisions concerning biological reproduction. As this report has already indicated the facilities have been provided for women to control their own fertility, and to alleviate familial pressures on women to reproduce early and many times and to ensure that plans for reproduction balance the resources and population of the collective productive unit rather than the individual household, collective decision-making processes have been suggested and experimentally

[1] "Reform of marriage and family system in China", PR, 13 Mar. 1964.

implemented. Where this is so women of the unit are encouraged
to meet and jointly plan and space their families thereby reducing
the controls and influence of the head of the household and other
family members.

The likely implications of these policies for the position of
peasant women were well advertised within China, and social
scientists abroad were also quick to foresee their likely repercussions for the redefinition of the female role. They argued
that by taking out the last vestiges of private land ownership and
management, the commune had destroyed the estate or economic basis
of the individual household.[1] The payment of wages to the
individual members instead of the household head, the expansion of
productive opportunities and their reorganisation on a collective
basis were all likely to favour the independence of women and the
reduction of the powers of the patriarch or male household head.[2]
It is undoubtedly true that these policies designed to reduce the
economic basis of the household and kinship groups have favoured
the redefinition of their position, but it can also be argued that
the traditional household structures remain largely unchanged in
rural areas and many socio-economic functions still accrue to
individual rural households. It is the structure and socio-
economic functions, accruing to individual households which have
implications for the sexual division of labour, reproduction and
the subordination and control of women.

The household

In both rural and urban areas the basic unit of domestic
organisation is the household or hu which was characterised in the
field situation as the group of kin relations bound by a common
budget and single kitchen. Virilocal marriage, or the recruitment
of wives to the domestic group in which husbands resided prior to
marriage, was widely practised before 1949 and nowhere are new rules
of post-marital residence explicitly stated. Although uxorilocal
marriage (matrilocal residence) was introduced in the recent movement to criticise Confucius and Lin Piao (1973-75) to promote the
equality of women,[3] virilocal marriage remains the norm in rural
China. Marriage thus immediately occasions the expansion of the
domestic group and the establishment of extended or joint families,
although it eventually also precipitates fission and its concomitant
economic partition. Normally however the latter takes place some
time after marriage and the formation of conjugal households was
coincident with household division rather than marriage. This
pattern is distinctive in rural areas, for in the cities young
couples tend to establish their own independent households on
marriage. Although the average size of rural households may seem

[1] M. Cohen: House united, house divided, Columbia, 1976,
p. 231; H. Lethbridge: "The communes in China" in Szcezepanik, E.F.
Economic and social problems of the Far East, Hong Kong, 1962,
p. 380.

[2] C. Yang: Communist society: the family and the village,
MIT, 1959, p. 39; W. Goode: World revolution and family patterns,
NY, 1963, pp. 301-2, 313.

[3] SWB, 30 Jan. 1975, 11 Feb. 1975.

little changed,[1] these mask a range and variation in size of any
one household at different points in its developmental cycle. At
any one time in the rural social field there are households who
take the conjugal or extended form depending on their stage in the
developmental cycle of the domestic group.[2] Moreover, it can be
argued that opportunities for the expansion of the rural household
have increased in latter years. Both Lang and Levy have noted
that in traditional China it may have been quite common for stem
families to maintain themselves for many years.[3] Poverty, poor
health and migration may have left many families with only one son
surviving to maturity in each generation. It seems likely now
that the improvements in diet, health and general welfare services
have increased the number of surviving sons and lengthened their
expected lifespan.[4] While opportunities for migration to the
cities remain very limited, there is evidence to suggest that
demographic factors have contributed to the new vertical and
horizontal proliferation of the generations in close proximity if
not within the same household. The maintenance and even expansion
of the traditional rural household can be attributed not only to
the survival of inherited forms but also to the new policies of
economic development which demand certain socio-economic functions
of the rural household.

Private property and land reform

Anthropologists who have studied the forms which the domestic
group took in traditional China have argued that the key factor in
its maintenance as a complex and extended form had been the
existence of landed properties or an estate sufficient in size to
meet the claims of its members.[5] The Communist Party too
identified private property as the primary economic foundation of
the domestic group and the abolition of the land component of the
estate has been a priority of the Government since the mid-1950s.
Prior to this, however, the Government had embarked on a policy of
land reform in the belief that the redistribution of land would give
all members of the household, and especially women, access to
ownership of the means of production and a new bargaining power
with which to redefine their subordinate position. Several articles
in the media at the time suggested that the redistribution of land
between and within households and new and equal inheritance laws
would create a source of economic independence for women.[6] However,

[1] Most past and present estimates number of the composition of
the household between four and six persons.

[2] See E. Croll: Chiang village: a household survey, CQ,
Dec. 1977, pp. 790-96.

[3] M. Levy: The family revolution in modern China, NY, 1949,
pp. 55-56; O. Lang: Chinese family and society, Yale, 1946, p. 10.

[4] See E. Croll: Chiang village: a household survey, CQ,
Dec. 1977, p. 793.

[5] M. Freedman: Chinese lineage and society: Fukien and
Kwangtung, London, 1966, p. 30; M. Cohen: 1976, p. 231.

[6] P's C, 1 June 1951; 1 Mar. 1953.

it may also be argued that land reform strengthened the property basis or the land component of the household estate and its exploitation maximised the functionality of the domestic group as a unit of production and with it the sanctions at the disposal of the household head rather than the resources at the command of women members. Within the rural household, individual claims to the land often remained more potential than real and often women who had little experience in organising agricultural production held the land in name only.[1]   The fact that women could bring with them a share of land in marriage or the household might be allocated a further portion of land on the marriage of one of its sons, only served to strengthen the resolve of the head of the domestic group to control the recruitment of women in marriage and consolidate its property base. It may be no coincidence that the period of immense hostility to the new Marriage Law with its provisions of free-choice marriage which resulted in the deaths of many women occurred at the same time as the property base of the rural household was strengthened through land reform.[2]   However, this situation was short-lived for it was somewhat altered by the collectivisation of agricultural land and its removal from the direct control of the individual household in the mid-1950s. The policies of collectivisation had the effect of reducing the land component of the individual family estate and the economic basis of the individual household, but certain socio-economic factors continue to be specific to the rural household.

Labour as a household resource

The economic organisation of China demands that the rural household continue to mobilise its resources in order to find solutions to a number of organisational problems, namely production and the transformation of materials for consumption. Despite the policies of collectivisation, the individual rural household is still a unit of production albeit greatly reduced in scope, and because community services are very unevenly distributed in rural areas it is also a primary unit of consumption. The economy of the domestic group no longer relies on the exploitation of the family lands or estate, but on the paid and unpaid labour of each member of the domestic group. In any society where labour forms the major part of the total means of production and where control over labour resources is the major source of social differentiation, the recruitment and biological reproduction of labour power itself is in constant demand. In both of these the role of women is crucial. Where the individual and private hiring of agricultural labour is prohibited by law as it is within the People's Republic of China, then the recruitment of women through marriage becomes one of the major means of expanding the labour power resources of the household and necessary for its reproduction.

In the rural areas, access to and organisation of labour is necessary to combine the three sectors of the economy: the income-earning contribution from the public sectors of the economy, the

---

[1] D. Davin: Woman-work: women and the Party in revolutionary China, Oxford, 1976: 116; E.J. Croll: Feminism and socialism in China, London, 1978.

[2] E.J. Croll: The negotiation of marriage in the People's Republic of China, Ph.D. Thesis, London, 1978, pp. 250-52.

sideline activities of the private sector of the economy and the non-remunerated contributions in the domestic sphere. In the collective sector of the economy, the income and welfare of the family is very much dependent on the ratio of wage earners to dependants within the household and whether the wage earners are male or female. In the private sector, the household is still an important unit for the production of its subsistence. The private sector includes not only private plots which comprise 4 to 5 per cent of the total area of collectively held land and is allocated on a per capita basis, but it also includes the raising of livestock such as pigs and chickens. By providing most of the vegetables and much of the meat for immediate consumption it composes a vital food resource as well as an important cash contribution to the household economy. Domestic labour involving the transformation of produce for consumption such as grinding corn, preserving vegetables, sewing and cooking and child care is an important unpaid contribution to the household economy which reduces the monetary costs of its maintenance. The performance of all these activities, collective, private and domestic relies on the distribution of the labour resources of the household between the three sectors and especially on the unpaid labour of women.

In each of the three sectors of the economy women's labour contributes to the maintenance of the household. In the collective sector, the women members of the household earn wages which are components of the family income and in the private sector pig and chicken raising have normally been defined as women's tasks. They often tend the private plots, but it is their unpaid domestic labour in the domestic sphere which remains crucial for the largely self-provisioning rural household. There have been a number of attempts to redefine the division of labour within the household. In the 1970s men have been encouraged to undertake an equal share of domestic labour. At the time of my first trip to China, the last meeting of men and women called by the local women's association in several villages had to do with the accommodation and sharing of domestic labour. Numerous role models have been published in the media of men who previously indulged in patriarchal attitudes and dismissed housework as women's work, but who have discarded these attitudes and now undertake their share.[1] But the same articles also suggested that the division of labour within the household had altered little both because of "limited material conditions and the influence of male supremacy".[2]

Despite these policies much of the domestic labour such as washing, mending, cooking and child minding is still regarded as women's work. At particular stages in a woman's life cycle her labour tends to be distributed in favour of the domestic and private sector. It is a common occurrence for the recruitment of a new daughter-in-law or wage earner in the collective sector to result in the release of the women of the older generation to manage the side-occupations of the private sector and undertake with the help of the younger generation domestic labour and child care. The maintenance of the household has as its base the exploitation of the unpaid labour of the women and to a greater extent of that of the women of the older generation. Indeed the extended composition of the household numbering more than one adult woman among its members alleviates to a degree "the double day" common in other societies.

[1] CR, June 1975.

[2] Hongqi, 1 Dec. 1973.

But women's unpaid labour is essential to the development of the rural economy in its present form with its low investment in community services and a certain siphoning off of its surplus for industrialisation programmes.

The recruitment of women

Several factors suggest that some policies to redefine the position of women have been modified over the years in the interests of maintaining the rural household as a unit of production and consumption and a concomitant control over its labour resources.

(a) One of the most common explanations or rationalisations given by the older generation in continuing to control the exchange of women in marriage contrary to the new ideology of free-choice marriage was cited in terms of their need to recruit additional labour power to maintain the household as an economic unit.[1] Parents would be "glad of a daughter-in-law's help" and exercised certain criteria to do with physical strength and conscientious work in making the choice of a spouse for their sons.

(b) The most common explanation for the persistence of the betrothal gift in rural areas, despite policies recommending its abolition in the interests of the independence and freedom of women, was that it took the form of compensation to the girl's family for the expenses of her upbringing and loss of her labour.[2]

(c) There is an apparent preference for the birth of sons in rural families, for only for them can daughters-in-law or additional labour power be recruited.

(d) An important factor influencing the age of marriage and the use of birth control, both of which are seen to be in the interests of women's health and their training and independence, was found to be the economic pressures in favour of the birth of a new generation of potential labourers. To maximise the resources of the rural household it aimed to ensure a steady supply of labour by incorporating the new generation or grandchildren into the labour force before the older generation or grandparents retired.[3]

(e) Because the rural household is a single unit of production and consumption it tends to have a single family budget to which all members contribute their wages and are reliant for their support. Normally this is managed by workers of the older generation and consequently may ensure the reliance of the younger on the older generation. This works against the economic independence and autonomy of both the younger male and female members of the household.

(f) Women were penalised in the public domain because of the sexual division of labour assigning them to domestic labour. Their annual and daily contribution to collective labour quotas was

---

[1] J. Chen: A year in Upper Felicity, London, 1973, p. 80; ZQ, 12 Feb. 1963.

[2] ZF, 1 Oct. 1963; ZQ, 19 Nov. 1964; NFRB, 25 Dec. 1964.

[3] GRB, 11 Sep. 1962; W.L. Parish: "Socialism and the Chinese peasant family", Journal of Asian Studies, Vol. XXIV, No. 3, May 1975, p. 618.

diminished in order to allow them time to undertake the unpaid servicing of the household. Policies introduced to encourage women to take part in political and collective decision making, many of which are part time and unpaid, have been jeopardised by the continuing household responsibilities of women and the distribution of their labour in favour of the private and domestic sectors at certain periods of their life cycle.

In contrast, in the urban areas there is no equivalent to the private sector of the economy, the household is less a unit of production and consumption and the number of community services available to urban women are far more numerous than in the rural areas. The contrast in the number of services available to rural and urban women may reflect the separate roles of agriculture and industry in the over-all economy. Despite the priorities given to agriculture in national development programmes, demands continue to be made on the agricultural surplus for capital formation and accumulation to contribute to the development of the industrial sector. The structure and function of the rural household has affected the demands made on the labour of women in rural areas and in a similar manner the maintenance of patrilocal kinship structures in rural China has affected the rules of marriage.

Women and kinship groups

Kinship groups have not only survived, but the inter-relationships within these groups have been formalised and institutionalised by the new demographic and economic policies of development. Although their land basis has been destroyed, there has been no large-scale rearrangement of the traditional distribution of rural persons, and rural areas continue to be characterised by discretely bounded villages which vary in size from a few tens to a few hundred households. These villages now have a new definition and function, and since the establishment of the communes they tend to coincide with the organisational levels of either the production team or production brigades depending on their size. But however it has been organisationally redefined, the spatial continuity of the village remains and it may coincide to a greater or lesser extent with particular kinship groups.

The proportion of kinship ties to other relations in the village may vary for those characteristic of the southern provinces such as Guangdong and Fujian, where single-surnamed village members comprise a single lineage, to the multi-surnamed villages of the northern provinces. In the past, the southern villages were dominated by lineages or large localised kin groups whose boundaries often coincided with those of the village, and evidence from the People's Republic of China suggests that lineage-based settlements continue to characterise much of southern China.[1] In the northern provinces the proportion of kin ties within the village had traditionally been less than in the south, but even in these there is some evidence to suggest that village exogamy was the rule thereby necessitating the movement and exchange of women.[2] Moreover, it

---

[1] J. Chen, 1973; N. Diamond: "Collectivisation, kinship and the status of women in rural China", Bulletin of the Concerned Asian Scholars, Jan.-Mar. 1975.

[2] M. Yang, 1945: 115.

may well be that demographic factors, especially the decline in
permanent physical mobility, or migration out, and the continuation
of patrilocal post-marital residence has increased the number of
agnatic or male-linked kin in these villages.   Apart from the
exchange of women in marriage, there is now little permanent movement between production brigades or villages and this very important
factor encourages a high level of involvement in kinship groups by
men.   In addition in both north and south China structural factors
which provide for the elaboration of male kinship groups have been
reinforced by the extent to which co-operation between villagers is
required to provide for and maintain the welfare of the rural
household which encourages a high degree of intimacy and frequence
of contact between kin.

A wide variety of functions formerly performed by the household
are now undertaken by the village which may compose a part of, an
entire or even several units of production, distribution and
accounting.   The time-honoured informal exchanges of goods and
services between neighbouring households has been institutionalised
and magnified by the process of collectivisation.   The inhabitants
of the villages are required to act together and co-operate on an
unprecedented level of exchange of goods and services.   The production team and production brigade are now units of production, the
owners of the means of production and the dominant units for the
organisation of labour within its boundaries.   Members of the
collectives are actively exhorted to solve common problems and to
mobilise common resources to improve the level of their services
through co-operation.   The structure and functions of kin groups
have had the effect of maintaining if not solidifying the bonds
between kinsmen.

In contrast the practice of surname and village exogamy means
that women often remain temporary members of their natal village
and become outsiders in their husbands' villages.   The following
factors suggest that this may work against the redefinition of the
role and status of women.

(a) In the organisation of production women are assigned to
the least skilled and least prestigious areas of production.   Women
make up the vast majority of agricultural workers of the production
team which requires less training and fewer skills than other
agricultural occupations.   The "temporary" and "outsider" nature
of their position does not encourage the investment in and training
of their skills or a redefinition of the sexual division of labour.
As daughters who are yet to marry out and wives married in, they
are often not encouraged to take up posts in rural industry or
develop scarce skills.   Men from the production team are much more
likely to be recruited into these activities than women.

(b) The numbers of women in leadership positions in rural
areas suggests that women have had a much more difficult time
breaking into the political decision-making processes where men are
permanent members of the production team and often also related
through kinship ties.   As temporary members they may not be sent
on training courses and as outsiders it takes them some time to
become familiar with a new political arena and build up their own
networks of support.

In contrast, in urban areas where there is a dispersal of kin
groups reducing the effects of surname exogamy, the individual and
wider choice of eligible mates, fewer norms of segregation and

neolocal post-marital residence, these factors all increase the
likelihood of a free-choice marriage and neolocal residence within
the urban neighbourhood.   This means that women are less likely
to be regarded as "temporary" or "outsider" members of their households and immediate neighbourhoods.   Marriage does not usually
affect the venue of a woman's occupation or her political
activities.

The reproduction of subordination: a summary

The introduction of a new ideology of equality, emancipation
or "liberation" was intended to redefine the relations between the
sexes within the household and kin groups.   The relations between
husbands and wives, between daughters-in-law and mothers-in-law
and between household members and senior male heads have all been
the subject of extensive ideological campaigns.   To no small
extent these have been instrumental in reducing the hierarchies
based on sex and generation, but at the same time as ideological
factors have been directed to redefine the relations within the
household and kin groups, demographic and economic factors have
been working to maintain, if not elaborate, their structures.   It
is the structure and functions of the household and kin groups
which have continued to reproduce the subordination of women in
rural areas in four main areas.

(a) So long as sons remain the only members of the household
and kin groups who will make a permanent contribution to the
economy of both and support their parents in old age, their value
cannot be matched by the temporary nature of daughters.   The birth
of sons remains an important source of prestige to women and
policies to control reproduction are not likely to have full effect
until the birth of at least one son per household.   The unequal
value of sons and daughters has been recognised in the recent
campaign to widely introduce matrilocal marriage in order to improve
the status of daughters.

(b) Women continue to be exchanged between households and
agnatic or male kin groups and their value in terms of the recruitment and reproduction of labour power has encouraged the permanent
members of households, men or older women, to place controls on
their movement in marriage.

(c) The maintenance of the household and the rural economy
relies on the unpaid labour of women.

(d) The training of young women in economic and political
skills is still a poor form of investment for local communities.

CHAPTER 6

Female solidarity groups

The establishment of female solidarity groups to safeguard the interests of women is beginning to be recommended as an important component of strategies to prevent developmental processes from becoming too prejudicial to their interests. In her cross-cultural analysis of the position of women in society, Peggy Sanday found there to be a high correlation between the presence of female solidarity groups devoted to female economic and political interests and female control over produce, demand or value placed on female produce and female participation in political activities.[1]

In China the very presence of a new separate formal and inde-pendent system of women's groups in itself marked a redefinition in the position of women and began to alter the local balance of power in the village and enterprises. Local solidarity groups were much more easily founded and tolerated if they were linked to practical objectives such as agriculture or handicrafts. For example, where the women's association had taught girls and women of the village a number of productive skills, the elders seeing them make good use of their time began to admit that "the women's association doesn't seem so bad after all. They're learning quite a lot that is useful there".[2] Local women's groups played an active role in encouraging women to enter social production and they normally became women's production teams in agriculture or handicraft co-operatives. Above all though they formed a new power base and acted as a source of confidence and strength from which women, individually and collectively, began to actively defend their newly won rights and interests. Time and again instances were recorded in which individual women turned to the newly formed solidarity groups for support in resolving a difficult and oppressive domestic situation. The establishment of female solidarity groups for the first time allowed women to contend patriarchal authority and the authority of the husband. Once there existed a source of power alternative to that of the tradi-tional patriarchal and village head power base of the men was directly threatened. The role of the female solidarity groups as an independent power base affecting domestic and village decisions was instrumental in establishing their value in the eyes of the village women. Their establishment also required women to speak out for themselves and learn to speak openly and to directly participate in public and political affairs. One village resident observed that within the women's association "brave wives and daughters-in-law, untrammelled by the presence of their men folk, could voice their own bitterness, encourage their sisters to do likewise and thus eventually hope to bring to the village-wide gatherings the strength of 'half of China'".[3] An anthropologist

---

[1] P.R. Sanday: "Towards a theory of the status of women", American Anthropologist, 1975, pp. 1,682-1,700.

[2] "The story of Tung Yulan", P's C, 16 Dec. 1954.

[3] W. Hinton, Fanshen, Vintage Books, NY, 1966, p. 157.

resident in a village in the 1950s noted that the very presence
of an independent organisation of women dealing with public affairs
was itself "a new phenomenon of considerable importance, something
entirely out of context with the traditional social order based
on the sexual division of labour and the exclusion of women from
public affairs".[1]

Within the women's movement, women might begin to think of
themselves as a separate and significant social category with
certain interests different from or even opposing those of men,
but the history of female solidarity groups has been marked by
certain ambiguities which surround their position as an independent
power base in a society in which the differences between social
classes and class struggle is viewed as the motivating force gene-
rating social change.   The history of women's subordination might
call for the separate organisation of women into their own
solidarity groups, but it was also argued that women did not form
a separate "class" however the term was defined.[2]   It has been
reiterated time and again that each sex was divided into classes
the nature of which primarily determined their social attitudes
and priorities.   Hence the Communist Party and the Government has
always demanded of the female solidarity groups that in addition
to improving the status of women they arouse an awareness of and
respond to all forms of oppression, class as well as patriarchal.
In the case of conflict the former was to take priority.   In
practice the uneasy alliance between the revolutionary and women's
movement has sometimes brought competing claims on the identity of
women, and the balance of these dual class and separate demands of
women directly affected the local histories of female solidarity
groups.

At certain periods during the last few decades local conditions
have favoured a strong group identity among women and the female
solidarity groups have forwarded the interests of women in a policy
of direct confrontation with the rest of the village.   In the
1940s when the initial acquisition of jural and economic and political rights immediately affected the balance of power in every
household, and where husbands and mothers-in-law persisted in their
opposition and ill-treatment there was some open and direct
struggle between the sexes.   Women felt that unless they actively
struggled against the men of their families they would not acquire
their new rights and many a recalcitrant or chauvinist husband was
brought before the village women's groups and publicly called upon
to explain his behaviour.[3]   However, in 1940 a Resolution of the
Woman's Organisations on Woman Work warned against isolating the
cause of women's liberation and unnecessary alienation of potential
support for their cause.[4]   In 1953 a general government directive
criticised the work methods used by many local women's groups in
their implementation of the Marriage Law of 1950.   It accused them
of interpreting the law almost exclusively in terms of women's

---

[1] C.K. Yang: A Chinese village in Communist transition, MIT,
1959, p. 178.

[2] Wen Mjuan: "How the problem of women should be viewed",
Hongqi, 28 Oct. 1964.

[3] J. Belden: China shakes the world, Gollancz, London, 1951,
pp. 316-7; W. Hinton: Fanshen, NY, 1966, p. 158.

[4] "Present woman work in rural districts of the liberated
areas" in documents of the women's movement, ACDWF, Peking, 1949.

rights and adopting an attitude of separatism and autonomy to directly generate antagonism between the sexes. The ensuing conflict between the apparently divided interests was reported to have caused disruption in village life, brought the new law into disrepute, isolated the active members of the women's groups and in some cases even led to the deaths and suicides of indivi-dual women.[1]

A more common trend in the villages however has been for women to display a weak group identity in the face of competing claims. Activists in the local women's groups often found them-selves on the defensive and arguing for the continued need for active solidarity to collectively give expression to their aspirations, protect their rights and interests and supervise the implementation of decrees and policies regarding the equality of men and women.[2] The continuing obstacles to their implementation and the sometimes limited definition of "emancipation" or "libera-tion" to mean mere entry into social production had caused some village groups to conclude that their goals had all but been achieved. They either lay dormant through lack of vitality and purpose[3] or were formally abolished when they were thought to be "no longer needed" as in Liuling village.[4] It was not unknown for local women leaders and activists to prefer to work in class associations, or what they considered to be the mainstream of economic and political activities, rather than in the apparently secondary or even diversionary women's groups concerned exclusively with the complications of the personal lives of women.[5] Resolutions on woman work have campaigned against the tendency among some men and women to think that all would be well with women so long as general revolutionary aims were fulfilled and that solidarity among women was at best secondary and at worst unnecessary.

Women in China have constantly been exhorted to act in defence of their interests and their failure to do so at all times may not be so much due to their failure to perceive the anomalies in their position, although at times this may be so, but due to the sometimes conflicting demands inherent in the very definition of solidarity for women in a class society. The ideology of solidarity may demand that differences between women due to age and position in household hierarchies and social class be de-emphasised in favour of unity within the female group, and in China the Government and the women's movement have remained divided over the question of whether women should primarily identify with members of their sex or with their class associates.

---

[1] "Directive of the Government Administrative Council con-cerning the thorough implementation of the Marriage Law", NCNA, 19 Mar. 1953.

[2] Teng Ying-chao: Speech in Report of the Eighth Party Congress, FLP, Peking, 1956; "In what respects should we be self-conscious", ZF, 1 Feb. 1962.

[3] I. and O. Crooks, 1966, p. 251.

[4] J. Myrdal: 1967, p. 239.

[5] "Conduct work among women in a more patient, thoroughgoing and attentive manner", RMRB, 8 Mar. 1962.

This division of opinion which had directly affected the ability of female solidarity groups to defend women's interests came to a head on the eve of the Cultural Revolution in 1966 and led to the temporary demise of the women's movement in China.

The Cultural Revolution

Prior to the Cultural Revolution, an article written in the Party magazine in 1964 entitled "How the problem of women should be viewed" analysed the present state of the women's movement.[1] It concluded that there was an acute internal struggle between those who thought that solidarity among women was paramount and those who thought that priority should be accorded to class solidarity. The controversy centred around whether the divisions between the sexes or those between the classes were the primary divisions in society. Was it possible to distinguish a single female or woman's as opposed to man's conception of life, and if so, were the widely disparate social attitudes of different classes of women sufficient to divide women one from another and cancel out the factors working for unity. Those who thought that women should primarily identify with their sex stressed the questions of physiology and distinguished a single woman's point of view on this basis. They concentrated on working out an authoritative view of reproduction, domesticity, marriage and child rearing. The critics of this point of view contended that to look at a single woman's viewpoint and distinguish her "special conception of life" was to recognise the existence of "abstract above-class" women, and this category, like that of "abstract above-class men", did not exist in this world. There was no single viewpoint to work out and defend.[2] The controversy between the two points of view threatened the very fabric of the Women's Federation, and this plus the tendency to think it had outlived its usefulness, the substantial movements to improve their jural, political and economic status in the 1950s, almost brought it to a standstill as a national and local functioning organisation. During the Cultural Revolution most of the local female solidarity groups fell into abeyance. The exact weighting which should be given to the various factors contributing to this situation is difficult to ascertain. How much it was the result of factors internal to the women's movement itself and how far it was at the behest of the Party's authority must remain as questions without answers in the present state of knowledge. We may have no special insights as to the whole question of the autonomy of the women's movement in this case, but what is certain is that the events of the Cultural Revolution in the mid sixties have been responsible for a reappraisal and re-evaluation of the benefits of solidarity among women in the 1970s.

During the Cultural Revolution there was no attempt to foster solidarity among women, rather the very definitions of class terms were elaborated to include attitudes to and by women and they were encouraged to raise their class consciousness through political study and participate in the current struggle between the proletarian and bourgeois classes. The organisation of women in the

---

[1] Hongqi, 28 Oct. 1964.

[2] ibid.

exclusive pursuit of their own rights and interests, and ideas such as "if men earned more women needn't work" and "somebody has to maintain the household so why not the women for men already have enough responsibility outside the home" were associated with the bourgeois class viewpoint and hence to be struggled against. There is some evidence that in the direct incorporation of women into the same political and vocational framework as men, women did play a more significant part in the events of the Cultural Revolution on a national and particularly at local levels than hitherto.[1] When the Swedish writer, Jan Myrdal, interviewed in one village seven years after his previous visit, he found that one of the greatest changes in the village was the attendance of women at the political meetings.[2] But there is much more evidence to suggest that in incorporating women's interests into the broader class definitions and the wider class struggle, with no special advocation or defence of their interests by the women's movement, the special interests of women were neglected.

At the national and local levels there was little attention given in the media to the position of women in society after the suspension of the Women's Federation and its magazine. Articles published in the media after the Cultural Revolution and my own interviews conducted in China in 1973 substantiate the impression that many individuals, associations and enterprises gave little attention to furthering women's interests. When the Revolutionary Committee (new management committees established during the Cultural Revolution) assumed over-all responsibility for the affairs of one county, they thought that cadres representing the interests of women's groups were unnecessary. They would involve women in all their work, but as a result women there found their special interests were ignored because the revolutionary committee had more work than it could possibly manage and there was no one person who was specifically charged to remind them of this responsibility.[3] Again from the same province, it was reported that local revolutionary committees either thought that anything they could do would have little bearing on the general position of women or they tended to assume that their over-all work would automatically see to the interests of women. They tended to generalise that "since work in every field included women there was no need to grasp woman work as a separate task".[4] In 1968, an article in a Shanghai newspaper had generally warned revolutionary committees against the new tendency that had arisen of "showing concern" for women without including the women themselves.[5] My own interviews indicated that women had come to recognise that although every field did include women, it was not enough to

---

[1] "Cadres in Honan Province", RMRB, 15 Nov. 1969.

[2] Myrdal and Kessle: 1973, pp. 111-118.

[3] Report of Revolutionary Committee, Lochang Xian, Guangdong Province, Hongqi, 1 Feb. 1971.

[4] Report of Writing Group of Hunan Provincial Committee, Hongqi, 1 Feb. 1971.

[5] "Role of women on revolutionary committees", Wenhui Bao, 14 June 1968.

include women in every field and neglect their special difficulties inherited from the past or their reproductive roles. It seems that it was their experience at the hands of revolutionary committees which re-established the value of solidarity among women and led to the rebuilding of local groups in the late sixties and early seventies.

In turning its attention to the creation of new solidarity groups among women, one commune described how it was responding to the demands of women and following a recent instruction from Mao Tse-tung who recommended anew that "it was still necessary to struggle against the concept of despising the women's movement because the people holding this concept fail to see its importance in redefining the role of women and the importance of their participation in the revolution".[1] The re-establishment of local female solidarity groups was officially encouraged, but they were reminded that they were not an area exempt from class struggle and that political study was essential to their participation in political decision making and representing the interests of their groups. One model brigade described how they and the women put these recommendations into practice.[2] First the leaders had met to discuss their own attitudes towards women's groups. In retrospect they thought that they had been too preoccupied with the general class struggle to pay attention to the interests of women. They revealed that they had thought that since they were busy with work of central importance they "must not allow women to drag their legs" and that "woman work really had no bearing on the general situation within the brigade". They held a meeting to criticise their tendency to slight or neglect the interests of women and to encourage the re-establishment of local women's organisations. At the same time the women of the brigade met to discuss their experience of the last few years and to reform their own groups and draw up their demands. These debates and discussions were published as an example to other brigades who also re-established their local women's groups. How far they were followed it is difficult to ascertain, but certainly by the time of my first visit to China in summer 1973, local women's groups had been reformed at the local levels with the avowed aims of both developing women's class interests and their interests as women.

Perhaps the most important principle to come out of the experience of the Cultural Revolution was the re-establishment of the interdependence between the women's movement and the Government to redefine the position of women. The functions of local solidarity groups among women is once again perceived to be two-fold in theory: to raise the consciousness of women both as members of a class and as women. The competing claims on the consciousness of women have once again been theoretically resolved by giving priority to the solidarity of women as members of a class on the grounds that without the establishment of socialist and proletarian interests there can be no substance to women's

---

[1] Report of Revolutionary Committee, Lochang Xian, Guangdong Province, Hongqi, 1 Feb. 1971.

[2] "Investigation Report of the Dongjin Brigade, Guangxi", Hongqi, 1 Feb. 1971.

liberation.[1]   At the same time there is a renewed emphasis and
evaluation of solidarity among women.   The recent campaign to
criticise Confucius and Lin Piao has gone some way to combine
both women's special and class interests in the one nationwide
movement, but how the dual demands and competing claims that
have characterised the history of local solidarity groups can
again be juxtaposed in practice when their interests conflict
remains to be seen.

What is important in the context of this report is that their
very revival as an independent power base is recognition by the
women themselves of their value in redefining the role and status
of women.   Their own experience confirmed for women the direct
correlation between the presence of female solidarity groups
devoted to their own socio-economic and political interests and
the furthering of those interests in society.   The difficulties
of combining the class interests of the Government and the special
interests of women in one struggle has produced a tension which
has directly affected women's ability to intervene on their own
behalf.   These groups have not always acted in defence of women's
interests or even defined clearly what these interests are, but it
was the direct experience of women that they were a great deal
worse off without them.

---

[1] "Talking of women's liberation", PR, 8 Mar. 1973;   "How we
women won equality", CR, Mar. 1975.

CHAPTER 7

The Chinese strategy: lessons in development

In recent years there is growing evidence that common patterns of development which are capital intensive, which mechanise production and introduce cash cropping are prejudicial to women.   In these conditions of rural development women have often been assigned to underdeveloped sectors of the economy or even separated from production altogether.   Indeed the continuing subordination of women may be unplanned and has often gone unnoticed.   It is within this context that governments, planners, agencies and feminists have been prompted to search for more effective and alternative strategies.   In this process, a growing interest has been focused on China, its goals of development and programmes designed to affect the integration of women, thus bringing into question the relevance of the Chinese experience in the formulation of alternative and effective policies.   Can other countries really imitate the Chinese development patterns under different ideological asuumptions, or adapt them to different political and social contexts?

It is probably not particularly valid to talk of an entire Chinese model in respect of women in that they have had no single encompassing blueprint for their strategy has been an evolving one. In devising many pragmatic solutions and shifting priorities as old problems remained and new problems arose, it has taken many twists and turns.   At the same time there is no doubt that certain key premises do underlie their strategy.   The major assumption of the Government in developing a strategy to redefine the position of women is that the goals of national and socialist development and the women's movement are interdependent.   The Communist Party has always assumed that there can be no redefinition of women's roles unless there is a socialist revolution and no transition to socialism unless women fully participate in the process of social change.   On this foundation the Government first mapped out a comprehensive and integrated programme which allowed for the development of a new (1) legal;   (2) material;   and (3) ideological base for the emancipation of women;   and (4) the growth of the women's movement to particularly forward their economic, social and political interests and redefine their domestic and public roles. Each aspect or component of this multi-faceted strategy is dependent on the achievement of another and it is the prior assumption that policies to end the subordination of women must be tackled as a whole and not piecemeal and with the pre-conditional establishment of socialist institutions which make it less likely that the experience of China can be directly transferable.   Yet there is no doubt that the history and experience of China in the last 25 years is certainly instructive in highlighting the problematic areas likely to be encountered in such a process of role and status redefinition.

In examining the working out of the strategies for both involving and benefiting women in the development process, this report has concentrated on the macrosocial, economic and political implications of their development experience in several broad areas.

(a) <u>Legislation</u>.   Progressive legislative changes may be a prerequisite to the redefinition of women's roles, but they mark not the culmination but only the beginning of a long process of social change including socio-economic and political changes. Legislation is by no means symbolic either of the degree to which a government is committed to the integration of women into development or their position in society.

(b) <u>Production and the sexual division of labour</u>.   Where a country is marked by a low level of the productive forces and it is agriculture which forms the main potential for and source of the accumulation of capital and industrialisation, there is more likely to be a greater competition for scarce resources.   This often means that despite a high commitment to the redefinition of the position of women, policies involving the allocation of resources such as the provision of community and welfare services and the reduction of the degree by which women's unpaid labour should subsidise the rural economy are hampered by a real or assumed shortage of capital. Without foresight and careful anticipatory planning, priorities made in the interests of short-term goals can easily become set as long-term policies to the detriment of women.

The reorganisation of the relations of production and the establishment of collective units of production into which women from the component households have been incorporated has facilitated the diffusion of certain benefits to women.   It has enabled the Government to mount extensive development programmes and to intervene in the interests of women by expanding productive opportunities for women in an already underemployed region, organise women separately, direct inputs into their teams and provide facilities for their education and training in agricultural skills, the improvement of their health and at least attempt to collectivise consumption and ease their individual household responsibilities.   However, the experience of China would also argue that the reorganisation of the relations of production must embrace the production and consumption activities of the household and thereby alter substantially the functions of and relations within the rural household.   In rural China it can be argued that not only have development policies maintained the household and kinship structures, but inadvertently they may also have been elaborated, which has had profound repercussions on the policies to redefine the sexual division of labour.

The Chinese experience would also suggest that while entry into social production may be a necessary condition for the redefinition of the position of women, it is clearly not a sufficient condition.   Other factors interfere with and discourage their access to and control over the strategic resources of society.

(c) <u>Ideology</u>.   Although this report takes issue with the current definition of the problem of women and rural development in China which is almost exclusively expressed in ideological terms, there is no doubt that ideologies, beliefs elaborated on women's supposed inferiority, self-abasement and dependence survived radical changes in the material circumstances of women in China.   To establish a new ruling ideology incorporating new definitions of women to replace those of male supremacy and female subordination has proved to be a necessary and arduous and difficult phase in the process of redefinition.   Although it can be argued very cogently that incomplete transformations in the mode of production encourages the persistence of certain ideological constraints in rural areas, even where there have been more complete transformations in the mode of production as in urban areas, the ideological constraints also persist albeit in a reduced form.

(d) <u>Female solidarity</u>. The early establishment of local women's solidarity groups and their separate work teams have played a key role in the strategy to redefine the position of women, in explaining the development process and incorporating women into it. It is in their own groups that women have gained at least the opportunity to acquire confidence and collective strength to begin to actively negotiate a new position for themselves. However, in a nationalist, revolutionary and socialist movement or country which is explicitly committed to redefining the position of women as part of the development process, there is a narrow line to tread between two opposing tendencies each of which may affect the history of the women's movement. One is to guard against thinking that the problem of women will take care of itself so long as general revolutionary aims are fulfilled and therefore attention accorded to the subject and the separate women's groups should on principle take a secondary place, and the second is the tendency by women to take an independent line on the redefinition of their role which is at variance with that of the Government and thus risk the intervention of the Party and State and the relegation of their interests to second place in the short or long term.

Finally, the question must be raised as to whether the degree of success achieved by the programmes in China warrant the attention and interest which they have attracted. Many problems in their definition and implementation remain and the present shortcomings in their position have been well documented both within China itself and outside its borders. At the same time as these are recognised, a comparison between the position of women in the past and in the present decade suggests that the role and status of women has indeed been redefined within a short time span as the result of a comprehensive and conscious strategy not typical of other developing countries. In sum, the experience of China argues for no short term and easy solution to both integrating and benefiting women by the development process. It does however add to an understanding of the complexity of the mechanisms of subordination and the means by which they are maintained and perpetuated. The Chinese themselves have often said that there are no blueprints for social change. Instead each phase has to be worked out, experimented with and analysed at each particular juncture, and perhaps it is just this history of working out, experimentation and self-conscious analysis which has marked out their experience as relevant to all those aiming to redefine women's contribution to and benefits from the development process.